How to Lead

PEARSON

At Pearson, we believe in learning – all kinds of learning for all kinds of people. Whether it's at home, in the classroom or in the workplace, learning is the key to improving our life chances.

That's why we're working with leading authors to bring you the latest thinking and best practices, so you can get better at the things that are important to you. You can learn on the page or on the move, and with content that's always crafted to help you understand quickly and apply what you've learned.

If you want to upgrade your personal skills or accelerate your career, become a more effective leader or more powerful communicator, discover new opportunities or simply find more inspiration, we can help you make progress in your work and life.

Pearson is the world's leading learning company. Our portfolio includes the Financial Times and our education business, Pearson International.

Every day our work helps learning flourish, and wherever learning flourishes, so do people.

To learn more, please visit us at **www.pearson.com/uk**

How to Lead

The definitive guide to effective leadership

4th edition

Jo Owen

PEARSON

Harlow, England • London • New York • Boston • San Francisco • Toronto • Sydney
Auckland • Singapore • Hong Kong • Tokyo • Seoul • Taipei • New Delhi
Cape Town • São Paulo • Mexico City • Madrid • Amsterdam • Munich • Paris • Milan

PEARSON EDUCATION LIMITED
Edinburgh Gate
Harlow CM20 2JE
United Kingdom
Tel: +44 (0)1279 623623
Web: www.pearson.com/uk

First published in Great Britain in 2005 (print and electronic)
Second edition published 2009 (print and electronic)
Third edition published 2011 (print and electronic)
Fourth edition published 2015 (print and electronic)

© Jo Owen 2005, 2009, 2011, 2015 (print and electronic)

The right of Jo Owen to be identified as author of this work has been asserted by him in
accordance with the Copyright, Designs and Patents Act 1988.

Pearson Education is not responsible for the content of third-party internet sites.

ISBN: 978-1-292-08362-9 (print)
      978-1-292-08364-3 (PDF)
      978-1-292-08363-6 (eText)
      978-1-292-08365-0 (ePub)

British Library Cataloguing-in-Publication Data
A catalogue record for the print edition is available from the British Library

Library of Congress Cataloging-in-Publication Data
Owen, Jo.
  How to lead : the definitive guide to effective leadership / Jo Owen. — 4th edition.
    pages cm
  Includes index.
  ISBN 978-1-292-08362-9 — ISBN 1-292-08362-X
  1. Leadership. 2. Management. I. Title.
  HD57.7.O946 2015
  658.4'092—dc23
                        2015013234

We are grateful fo[...] rtfolio Matrix
from the Product Portfolio Matrix, © 1970, The Boston Consulting Group (BCG).

10 9 8 7 6 5 4 3 2 1
19 18 17 16 15

Cover design by Nick Redeyoff

Print edition typeset in 10/14 Plantin by 76
Print edition printed by Ashford Colour Press Ltd, Gosport

NOTE THAT ANY PAGE CROSS REFERENCES REFER TO THE PRINT EDITION

Contents

About the author

Jo Owen practices what he preaches as a leader. He has worked with over 100 of the best (and one or two of the worst) organisations on the planet. He was a partner at Accenture and started a bank.

He is a founder of eight charities with a combined turnover of over £100 million annually, including Teach First which is the largest graduate recruiter in the UK. Jo is a top corporate coach and speaker on leadership, and is the bestselling author of *How to Manage, How to Sell, How to Influence and The Mobile MBA*. He can be reached at jo@ilead.guru.

Acknowledgements

Creating this book has been a personal journey of discovery, in the course of which I have met many old and new guides to help me along the way. I would not have even started the journey without the inspiration of the staff and participants of Teach First: if they are the leaders of the future, our future is in good hands. Since its creation 13 years ago, Teach First has become the largest graduate recruiter in the UK: a great example of leadership in action. I hope this book helps all the Teach First participants on their journeys towards leadership.

I would not have had the courage to start the book without the gentle support of my agent, Frances Kelly, and of Richard Stagg and Christopher Cudmore of Pearson.

In the course of researching *How to Lead* I have drawn on the time and support of many people. A vast array of staff and participants at Teach First, Future Leaders and Teaching Leaders has been a live laboratory for testing the ideas in *How to Lead*. I am also hugely grateful to the several thousand people I have interviewed on video or talked to informally, or who have replied to questionnaires. Readers of the last three editions have pitched in with practical ideas, challenging questions and personal experiences. My only regret is that I cannot include all the material I have been offered. Finally, my thanks go to the 100-plus organisations I have worked with over the years. I certainly have learned much from them – I hope they got something in return.

Leaders, like authors, learn to take responsibility. So blame for the failings of the book lie with me, not with the wonderful support I have received from so many current and future leaders.

About the fourth edition

The reaction to the first three editions of *How to Lead* showed great hunger for discovering about leadership as it is for mortals. The basic idea of this book is that anyone can learn to lead, and that everyone can learn to lead better. Leadership is like sport or music: we may not be global megastars, but we can all improve with practice and guidance. We can at least be the best of who we are.

The fourth edition is a large step forwards from the first three editions. It follows the previous editions with a relentless focus on the practical skills of leadership. But this edition now also focuses on what leaders have to do to be effective: it marries actions to skills.

Continuing research on leadership over the ten years since the first edition has shown that there is a consistent set of actions that leaders have to follow at all levels of the organisation. This can be summarised as IPA: Idea, People, Action. The best leaders have a clear idea of how they are going to make a difference; they assemble a great team to make the difference; and then they make it happen. This sounds obvious. Like most things that are obvious, many managers never see it, and even fewer are able to put it into practice. This book shows how practising managers and leaders at all levels put the obvious into action.

Recent research has shown that besides the right skills and actions, the best leaders need one more vital ingredient to succeed: the right mindset. Put simply, the best leaders act differently from the rest because they think differently. Understanding the mindset difference has been a major research focus over the last five years and the results are summarised in a new section in this edition. The good news is that the success mindset is consistent across all leaders and that we can all learn it if we want to.

As with previous editions, this book draws on original research across public, private and voluntary sectors. Traditionally, most leadership books are based on private sector examples. This is massive myopia. Having set up eight national charities (including the largest graduate recruiter in the UK, Teach First), I am acutely aware of the challenges that voluntary sector leaders face. They have minimal resources compared with the private sector: that does not make their task easier. And public sector leadership is not easy street either – huge constraints and intense scrutiny are just a couple of the challenges public sector leaders face. Each sector can learn from the others. Having said that, the required skills and actions of effective leaders remain the same across all sectors. The principles of leadership are universal, but how you apply them is unique to your context.

As with the earlier editions, you cannot read this book and finish it as a leader. But it will help you put structure on the random walk of experience; it will help you make sense of the nonsense around you; it will help you accelerate your learning; and it can be your private coach on your path to leadership.

Introduction

Leadership is too often shrouded in mystery. To become leaders we are urged to become a combination of Genghis Khan, Nelson Mandela, Machiavelli and Gandhi. A few people feel they are already that good. The rest of us feel slightly small when measured against such giants.

The mystery deepens when you try to define what makes a good leader in practice. We can all recognise a good leader in our daily lives. But no leader seems to conform to a single template.

Some academics and consultants decided to solve the mystery of leadership. They had time on their hands – they were on safari. By way of a warm-up exercise they decided to design the perfect predator. Each took responsibility for one element of the predator. The result was a beast with the legs of a cheetah, the jaws of a crocodile, the hide of a rhino, the neck of a giraffe, the ears of an elephant, the tail of a scorpion and the attitude of a hippo. The beast promptly collapsed under the weight of its own improbability.

Undeterred, the group turned their attention to designing the perfect leader. Their perfect leader looked like this:

- creative and disciplined
- visionary and detailed
- motivational and commanding
- directing and empowering

- ambitious and humble
- reliable and risk taking
- intuitive and logical
- intellectual and emotional
- coaching and controlling.

This leader also collapsed under the weight of overwhelming improbability.

The good news is that we do not have to be perfect to be a leader. We have to fit the situation. The polar bear is the perfect predator in the Arctic but would be useless in Papua New Guinea. Winston Churchill had to endure what he called his 'wilderness years' in peacetime. He just happened to be perfect as a wartime leader. The same leader enjoyed different outcomes in different situations.

> The good news is that we do not have to be perfect to be a leader.

How to Lead is about becoming an effective leader, not the perfect leader.

In search of the pixie dust of leadership

There has been a long search for the alchemy of leadership: we all want to find the elusive pixie dust that we can sprinkle on ourselves to turn us into glittering leaders.

Over ten years of research for this book more than 1,000 individuals helped by identifying what they saw as effective leadership at all levels of their organisations. In addition, more than 50 CEO-level individuals in the public, private and voluntary sectors, in both small and large organisations, gave in-depth interviews. If anyone knows about the pixie dust, they should. I also reviewed 30 years' experience of working with over 100 of the world's best, and one or two of the world's worst, organisations to see what patterns of leadership emerged. Over the past seven years I have even worked with traditional societies from Mali to Mongolia and the Arctic to Australia by way of Papua New Guinea to see how they are led. Closer to home, I led a study for Oxford University of Anglo–French leadership to discover how far the world of the leader changes when you cross the Channel.

The bad news is that leaders have no pixie dust. Or if they do, they are hiding it very well. But there is plenty of good news:

● Everyone can be a leader. The leaders we talked to came in all sorts of flavours and styles and all had different success formulas.

● You can load the dice in your favour. There are some things that all leaders do well. It does not guarantee success, but it does make success more likely.

● You can learn to be a leader. You do not have to be someone else – you do not have to become Napoleon or Mother Teresa – you simply have to be the best of who you are.

This book shows how you can acquire the habits of effective leaders and how you can adapt them to your own style.

Unravelling the mysteries of leadership

Leadership is inundated by small words with big meanings, such as *vision* and *values* and *integrity*. It is a subject that suffers from an extraordinary amount of hype and nonsense. In my exploration of leadership the mysteries began to melt away. The leaders gave reassuringly practical answers for some common questions about leadership:

● Can you learn to be a leader?
● What is this vision thing?
● Do values have any value in reality?
● How do leaders with apparent weaknesses succeed?
● Why do some great people fail as leaders?
● What do leaders look for in their followers?

- What makes a good leader?
- Is a leader just the person at the top?
- How do you handle conflict and crises?

What follows is not a theory of leadership, it is the collected wisdom of people who are leading at all levels in different types of organisations. The result is a book that can act as your coach to being an effective leader wherever you may work.

In search of any leadership

The search for leadership started with an easy question: what is leadership? This promptly lost everyone in a jungle of conflicting views expressed both forcibly and persuasively. Everyone recognises a good leader when they see one, but no one agrees on a common definition.

> 'Leadership is about taking people where they would not have got by themselves.'

I found the most useful definition came from Henry Kissinger: 'Leadership is about taking people where they would not have got by themselves.' This seems simple, even obvious. But it has big implications:

- The person at the top of the organisation may be in a leadership position, but they may not be leading. They may be careful stewards of a legacy organisation.
- You can be a leader at any level of the organisation. Leadership is not about seniority or your title, it is about what you do.
- Leaders need followers. You may be smarter than Einstein, but if no one is following you, you cannot be a leader.

If seniority is a dead end for defining leadership, so are qualifications. A quick look at the ten richest self-made billionaires on our planet shows that a degree is not required for success. Of the top ten at the end of 2014, six of them had no degree: Amancio

Ortega, Larry Ellison, Bill Gates, Mark Zuckerberg, Sheldon Adelson and Li Ka-shing. Only Michael Bloomberg has been troubled by having an MBA. You may need to be smart, but you do not need a piece of paper to prove it.

So if leadership is not about seniority or formal qualifications, surely a good leader must be skilled? This is, at best, partly true. A skilled leader is normally better than an unskilled leader. But look at the leaders where you work. They may not be the most skilled. Indeed, as they rise, so they appear more in the spotlight and their weaknesses become clearer to everyone. And this is what the leaders themselves recognised in interviews: they know they lack some core skills. If they are not good at accounting, they hire an accountant. If they don't know the law, they hire a lawyer. For them, leadership is a team sport. As a leader, you do not have to be good at everything, but you have to be good at something.

All of this is remarkably good news for anyone who wants to lead. Through this fog of confusion about leadership, we have made several important discoveries:

- You can lead at any level of the organisation.
- You do not need qualifications to lead.
- You do not need to be perfect to lead: no one gets ticks in all the boxes.

But still we need to find the pixie dust that separates out the leaders from the followers. Following Sherlock Holmes' principle that once you have discounted everything else, what remains must be the answer, we can start to tease out the truth about leadership.

The IPA agenda

I decided to look at what leaders actually do. Day to day, they do what most of us do. They go to meetings, talk to people, deal with crises, get fed up with email and work long hours. In any one day it is hard to see a pattern to their work. Look at what they do over a month or a year and it soon becomes clear that their apparently random or routine meetings and messages have a clear pattern.

The best leaders focus on just three priorities, which form the IPA agenda: Idea, People, Action.

> The best leaders focus on just three priorities: Idea, People, Action.

First, leaders at all levels have a very simple idea. We can call it a strategy if we want to be sophisticated, or a vision if we want to be aspirational. Behind every great business of any size there is normally a great, and very simple, idea. For instance:

- P&G: building great brands.
- Microsoft: dominating desktop operating systems.
- Facebook: connecting friends.
- Toyota: quality as reliability.
- Shazam: identifying the music you are listening to.

Each idea may be very simple, but making it happen is very hard. The idea serves to focus the energy and resources of each firm; it gives clarity and direction to staff and provides a viable way of competing and succeeding in the marketplace. The idea is not the formal vision, mission strategy or even strategic intent of the firm – we can leave the wordsmithing to top management and consultants – the idea is what in practice binds and drives the firm. We will see how leaders at every level can have an idea that works for them.

The second part of the IPA agenda is people. Leaders do not act alone. They make things happen through other people. And that means that the best leaders attract, motivate and empower the best teams. As a leader, you are only as good as the team you build around you. Do not assume that the team you inherit is the team you need in the future. You have to build a team that can turn your idea into reality – that means finding the people with the right skills and the right values. Normally, it is easy to find the right skills but much harder to find the right values. Do not compromise on either the skills or the values.

The final part of the IPA agenda is action. I found that the best leaders separate the noise from the signal very well. In the day-to-day noise of crises, conflicts, random requests, setbacks and surprises it is easy to lose the signal, to lose sight of what you must achieve: the urgent drives out the important. The best leaders deal with the noise but make sure they find time to keep pushing forward with their idea – they have a keen sense of priorities.

This IPA agenda is so important, for leaders at all levels, that it forms the basic structure of the book. No matter where you are, if you follow the IPA agenda you are likely to become a more effective leader.

The three pillars of leadership

The IPA agenda is simple, but it is just the first of the three pillars of leadership. Focusing on the actions of a leader is to focus on symptoms, not causes. We can see what leaders do, but we have to dig deeper to find out why they are so effective in what they do.

The second pillar of leadership came from asking people what they wanted from the leaders where they work. Asking people what they want is a pretty simple idea in business, but it has rarely been done in the world of leadership. The answers were a revelation. But before you read on, think about what you want from your boss and what you expect from leaders at each level.

If you want to be a leader who attracts great followers, then it pays to know what your followers expect from you. What people want from leaders is a set of leadership behaviours. It is not about what you do, it is about how you are.

> What people want from leaders is a set of leadership behaviours.

Here are the key behaviours expected of a leader at the top:

- ability to motivate others
- vision
- honesty and integrity
- decisiveness
- ability to handle crises.

It is worth reflecting for a moment on what is not on the list: management skills, reliability, intelligence, ambition, attention to detail, planning and organisation all failed to register. As this leadership journey unfolds, we will explore what the expected behaviours of a leader really mean. We will also discover how we can display these behaviours effectively.

At this point it was tempting to declare victory. But the list did not look right. What we expect of top leaders is not necessarily the same as what we expect of emerging leaders. The 1,000 volunteers who helped in the search for leadership confirmed this suspicion. The behaviours they valued in emerging leaders were totally different from the behaviours they expected in senior leaders, as shown in the table below.

Expected behaviours of leaders at all levels

Top leaders	Leaders in the middle	Recent graduates/ emerging leaders
Vision	Ability to motivate others	Hard work
Ability to motivate others	Decisiveness	Proactivity
Decisiveness	Industry experience	Intelligence
Ability to handle crises	Networking ability	Reliability
Honesty and integrity	Delegation	Ambition

We will explore what these behaviours mean and how you can learn them in the course of this book. At this point, the important thing to note is that the rules of survival and success change as your career progresses. To start off with, you need qualities such as hard work and reliability. These may seem like low hurdles to leap, but they trip up many people. At first, you can succeed by doing the basics well.

The risk comes with your first promotion. You will have learned a success formula based on hard work, reliability and being proactive. You will naturally be inclined to stick to your success formula and redouble your efforts. That way, disaster looms. As you head into middle leadership, you need different skills. You are no longer the player on the pitch making all the runs and the tackles, you are the coach on the side, selecting, developing and directing the best team – that is a completely different skill set for you to learn.

As you climb the career mountain, the view changes. You no longer see the day-to-day detail at the bottom of the mountain, you take a larger and longer view of what is important. That in turn means learning new skills and behaviours.

The best leaders are always learning and adapting; average leaders stick to a tried-and-tested success formula and soon find that they plateau out. Learning means trying new ways of working, doing new things. That inevitably carries the risk of setbacks, which means that the best leaders have courage to try things; they need resilience to deal with setbacks when they come along. The word failure does not cross their minds, they simply see each setback as a chance to learn and to grow stronger.

The need to keep on learning and growing hints at the third pillar of leadership on which this book is based. Behaviour does not come out of nowhere. It comes from the way you think. Over the last five years, the main focus of my leadership research has been to find out whether the best leaders act and behave differently because of the way they think.

> Behaviour does not come out of nowhere. It comes from the way you think.

It is clear that there is a distinctive leadership mindset. Like skills and behaviours, it is something anyone can learn. The seven mindsets of success are:

- Be positive, not hokey.
- Aim for the stars: have high expectations.
- Believe in yourself or no one else will.
- Learn and grow.
- Be brave: accelerate your career.
- Stay the course while others fall.
- Be ruthless, selectively.

On a good day, we all exhibit most of these mindsets. The best leaders keep this mindset on bad days as well as good, every day of the year. And they take the mindset further than most of us – they take bigger risks, are ready to be more ruthless and yet are more positive than most. How they cultivate this mindset is explored in Part 3 of the book.

The nature of leadership

1 **Everyone can learn to lead, and to lead better**
You do not have to be born to lead. Leadership is based on skills everyone can and should learn. You can learn from good and bad role models and experience. Never stop learning.

2 **No leader is perfect**
No leader gets ticks in all the boxes. Do not strive for perfection – strive for improvement and build on your strengths.

3 **You can lead at any level**
Leadership is about performance, not position. If you take people where they would not have gone by themselves, you are leading.

4 **Build on your strengths**
All leaders have a unique signature strength that lets them succeed in the right context. Build on your strengths, work around weaknesses.

5   Leadership is a team sport
    Do not try to be the lone hero. Work with others who have strengths
    that are different from yours and will compensate for your gaps.

6   Make a difference
    Do not accept the status quo. Leaders push themselves and others
    to over-achieve, to go beyond their comfort zone and to develop
    themselves and their organisation.

7   Find your context
    Leaders who succeed in one context can fail in another. Find out where you
    can use your signature strengths to best advantage if you want to succeed.

8   People and political skills become more important with seniority
    Technical skills are enough to gain promotion at junior levels. The more
    senior you become, the more you must master the arts of managing
    people and managing politics.

9   The rules of leadership change at each level of the organisation
    Success at one level does not lead to success at the next level.
    Expectations change – learn those expectations and develop new skills
    to meet the new expectations.

10 You are responsible
    You are responsible for your performance, your career and your feelings.

Learning to lead

It is one thing to describe leadership, it is another matter to learn
it. Too often, leadership is exemplified by the great men (nearly
always men) of business and of history.
This is not helpful to normal human
beings. Nor is it practical. We could not
all become Genghis Khan or Steve Jobs,
even if we wanted to. And a firm full of
Genghis Khan wannabes would not be a
happy place. So you cannot succeed by trying to become someone
else. But equally, you cannot succeed by just being yourself. If you

> You cannot succeed
> by trying to become
> someone else.

hang around like a teenager in full hormonal angst waiting for the world to recognise your innate genius, humanity and talent, you are likely to be in for a long wait.

So if you cannot succeed by becoming someone else, and you cannot succeed just by being yourself, what is the way forward? The way to success is by becoming the best of who you are. All the leaders we spoke to were clear that they succeeded by building on their strengths. Everyone has weaknesses – but building on weakness is not a recipe for success. Not many Olympic athletes win gold by focusing on their weaknesses – you would not ask a weightlifter to work on their weakness in synchronised swimming. Not many leaders succeed by focusing on their weaknesses either. You do not need to try to be someone else, you simply need to be the best of who you are. Build on your strengths and work around your weaknesses.

> **This book does not guarantee success, but it will load the dice in your favour.**

This book is your guide to the leadership journey. It focuses on the many practical skills that help distinguish effective from less effective leaders. It does not guarantee success, but it will load the dice in your favour.

There is some debate on whether you can learn to lead, and if so, how. The good news is that everyone can learn to lead to some level of proficiency, just as we can all learn to play a musical instrument or play a sport. We may not land up being the greatest musician, sportsperson or leader, but at least we can be a better one.

The alternative theory, that leaders are born, not bred, is terrifying. England tried this theory for roughly 900 years when the monarchy and aristocracy ruled by right of birth. The result was that for 900 years the country was led by murderers, rapists, kleptocrats, madmen, drug runners and the occasional genius who was meant to make up for the rest. Applying the same theory to business does not bode well: most family businesses discover that the saying 'clogs to clogs in three generations' holds true. The first generation makes the money, the second generation spends it and the third is back to where the first generation started.

Believing that leaders are born, not bred, is fatalistic. You may as well give everyone a DNA test when they start their careers and let that determine their fate. In practice, we can help everyone improve their leadership potential. The only question is how. To test this, we asked our leaders how they learned to lead. We let them choose two ways of learning from the following six:

● books

● courses

● peers

● bosses (good and bad lessons)

● role models (in and beyond work)

● experience.

Before looking at the answer, you may want to think which two sources of learning have been most important to you. Having tried the same question with thousands of executives around the world, there is a uniform answer. No one claims to have learned mainly from books or courses. This could be bad news for someone who writes books and leads courses. We all learn either from direct experience or from the experience of others around us. These are the lessons we value most.

The problem with learning from experience is that experience is a random walk. If you are lucky, you bump into good experiences, bosses, peers and role models. If you are unlucky, you get poor experiences, bosses, peers and role models. You can hope to get lucky with your random walk. But luck is not a strategy and hope is not a method. You need to manage your journey to leadership. And that is where the books and courses help. You cannot start at page 1 of a book and finish at page 250 as a leader – that is not the point of books or courses. They help you make sense of your

Luck is not a strategy and hope is not a method.

experiences, help you remove some of the randomness from the random walk of experience and help you accelerate your path to leadership. *How to Lead* provides you with frameworks to support your learning from experience: it is a structure on which you can build your journey to success.

Part 1

Idea: set your direction

Introduction

Our journey starts with an idea: not any idea, but your idea about your future perfect. Once you have this, you have your lodestar, which can guide you, focus your efforts, shape your team and give you your claim to fame. The greatest leaders have the greatest ideas. Anyone at any level can have a distinctive idea which drives their team forward. A good idea lets you lead, whatever your title or role may be.

Part 1 of the book shows how the power of a good idea separates leaders from managers, and how you can develop your idea of a future perfect whatever role you may have now. But it is not enough to have an idea. You have to show that it is relevant, worthwhile and actionable. You have to communicate and sell the idea to your team, bosses and peers. And you have to know how to make the idea work alongside the formal strategy of your workplace, which means navigating the world of strategy comfortably.

By the end of Part 1, you should be more comfortable about defining, evaluating and selling your future perfect idea. It is this that shapes your future, so it is the natural starting point for the book. Parts 2 and 3 will show how you can convert your idea into reality through a great team and by mastering the art of making things happen in a complex world.

The starting point is to understand why ideas are so powerful and how they define success and failure.

Chapter 1

The power of ideas

The test of a good leader is whether they can take people where they would not have got by themselves. This is true if you lead a giant organisation like Google, or if you lead a team of five or six people. You have to have an idea about how you will make a difference. You have to create a future that is different and better. There is nothing wrong with sustaining and gradually improving the situation you inherited – that is what all managers have to do. But as a leader you have to do more than just manage. Instead of sustaining a legacy from the past, you have to create a legacy for the future.

> Create a future that is different and better.

Having a clear idea about how you will create a better future sounds obvious, but it is often lost in the daily battle to survive. We may want to change the world, but right now we have a customer screaming down the telephone, the month end close is due in two hours, there is the presentation to prepare and 100 emails to deal with. As a leader, you have to deal with the day-to-day battles but never lose sight of the greater goal you want to achieve.

Think about your position. What will be different in one or two years' time as a result of your leadership? Of course, you will have various budget and performance goals to meet. If you are an effective manager you will meet those goals; if you are unlucky you may struggle. But beyond meeting your management objectives, how will things be different and better, in a way that other people will remember and remark on?

Making a difference is genuinely difficult. As an exercise in leadership classes I ask groups to name each British prime minister or US president since the end of the last World War. I then ask them to recall one thing about each leader, other than the foreign wars they engaged in. Take a look at the box to see how British prime ministers are typically remembered.

How British prime ministers are remembered in leadership workshops

- Attlee: introducing the welfare state.
- Churchill: nothing as a peacetime leader, in vivid contrast to his wartime years.
- Eden: Suez Canal debacle.
- Macmillan: saying 'You've never had it so good'.
- Douglas-Home: most groups have never even heard of this leader.
- Wilson: talking about the 'white heat of the technology revolution' in the 1960s, although no one is quite sure what technology or what revolution he was talking about.
- Heath: sailing, and taking the UK into the European Community.
- Wilson (again): smoking pipes.
- Callaghan: strikes, blackouts and the three-day working week.
- Thatcher: Thatcherism and much positive and negative besides.
- Major: a Spitting Image puppet showing him wearing underpants outside his trousers.
- Blair: the Iraq war.
- Brown: the financial crisis.
- Cameron: too early to say.

As you look at the list of prime ministers, there are some striking lessons. Most of these great leaders who dominated the media for years are remembered for very little. Only two of them are remembered how they would want to be remembered: Attlee for creating the welfare state and Thatcher for Thatcherism. Even Churchill in peacetime was completely forgettable, and one prime minister is so obscure that no one remembers he was prime minister (Douglas-Home).

The two prime ministers who are remembered had a very clear idea of how they wanted to change the country, and they succeeded: they changed the country on their terms. It is not clear what the others really wanted to achieve, other than gaining power and keeping their opponents out of power. Doubtless they had great plans in their heads and fought huge political battles in their time, and they probably convinced themselves that they made a difference. But the verdict of history is unforgiving: most of them failed as leaders.

Now apply the prime minister test to yourself. How will you be remembered? It is genuinely difficult to be remembered, let alone thanked, for anything. Think back on the various bosses and CEOs you have had: how did they make a difference and what do you remember them for? The chances are you remember them for how they were, not for what they did. You will remember how they treated you and how they behaved, not whether they beat budget by 7%.

> If you want to lead, you have to make a difference.

If you want to manage, you can manage the role you inherited and seek to improve it. That is hard work in itself. If you want to lead, you have to make a difference. You need an idea that others will notice and remember. As we shall see in the next chapter, a compelling idea will help you and your team perform much better.

Chapter 2

Why your idea matters

You need a compelling idea of the future for four reasons:

1 To gain control over your business or unit.
2 To create a clear sense of priorities: what you will and will not do.
3 To give hope and purpose to your team.
4 To demonstrate you are making a difference.

Gain control over your business or unit

It is a common mistake to believe that if you have been put in charge you are in control. We have already seen that leadership is not about your title, it is about what you do. If you are put in charge of a unit but do not have your own clear agenda, then you are not in full control – you are at the mercy of every new initiative that comes from on top, and of all the conflicting goals and priorities that afflict any place of work.

Once you have a clear idea about how you want to make a difference, you can set your agenda and take control. You can rebuild your team so that you have the right mix of skills in place to make the difference; you can start to set priorities and allocate resources;

you can decide what you need to change and how the team needs to work. You will no longer be drifting with the tide of corporate events, rather you will start to swim in a direction you choose. You will be in control. Control is the difference between leading and drifting.

Control is not about micro managing: if you control usage of the photocopier, you are probably controlling the wrong thing. Micro management is often used by weak managers as a substitute for real leadership. It gives the appearance of being in control, without the risk of actually making a decision about where you want to focus and where you want to lead the team. Control means setting the direction, building the team and then empowering and supporting the team to achieve that goal. Let go of the photocopy machine and focus on what counts.

Create a clear sense of priorities: what you will and will not do

How many people think they have too few goals that are too easy to achieve? Not many. The world of work is not getting any easier. As firms become fitter and flatter, more pressure is piled on leaders within the firm. They face conflicting goals: goals from on top and the need to collaborate and occasionally compete with colleagues in other departments.

Most people can cope with pressure, and some thrive under it. But few people cope well with stress for long. The difference between pressure and stress is control – if we have to achieve a goal but we are in control of our destiny, then we can rise to the challenge. Now remove the control: make our goal dependent on other people, throw in random last-minute demands from bosses and peers, suddenly remove a key resource, find the deadline has been brought forward arbitrarily and we lose control of our fate, and our stress levels soar.

> The difference between pressure and stress is control.

Once you have a clear agenda, you start to gain control. You have a basis on which to say no to work that is not important; you can start to focus time and effort on those things that matter most. No one ever has 100% control, but that is not an argument against trying to take some control. In a world of endless ambiguity, we need to create as much clarity as we can. If we have no agenda, no idea, then we have no clarity or control. A clear agenda is a good first step towards gaining some control.

Give hope and purpose to your team

When we asked people what they wanted from a good boss, we also got plenty of feedback about what makes a bad boss. One thing that drove interviewees to distraction was bosses who could not make decisions and changed their minds. This is hugely demoralising for the team: it means uncertainty, confusion and endless rework. The rework comes about each time the leader changes their mind, and is the result of a lack of clarity about the team's direction.

Followers want a leader with a clear sense of direction. They want to believe that they are working towards a better future – they expect a leader to give clarity, hope and purpose to their work.

The world is becoming more complicated and there is much talk of 'managing complexity'. You need to be smart and work hard to manage complexity. But you need to be even smarter to create simplicity out of complexity, to create the clarity and the focus that your team craves. If you have a clear idea about what you want to achieve, then you can create the clarity your team wants.

Demonstrate you are making a difference

Think back to the prime minister test. All the prime ministers will have convinced themselves that they were making a difference and earning their place in the history books. But they were not making a difference that was noticed.

If you want to be seen as a leader, you have to be seen to make a difference. This is a tough test to pass. We can all believe we are making a difference, but who will believe us? To test whether you are making a real difference, try answering the following questions:

- Will a boss two levels up from me notice what I am doing?
- Do colleagues in other departments think I am making a difference?
- How will I remember this year in ten years' time?

Rest assured that meeting your KPIs (key performance indicators) or beating your budget target by a few per cent will not pass these tests.

Even at the most senior levels, leaders need to have a simple story to tell to the board, their customers and stakeholders. A lovingly crafted 80-page PowerPoint presentation will be remembered by no one. As a test, what is the simple idea behind the following: Google, Microsoft, Rolls-Royce automobiles, Lidl? They doubtless have huge and detailed strategies and planning documents, but all are driven by a very simple idea:

> Leaders need to have a simple story to tell to the board, their customers and stakeholders.

- Google: paid search.
- Microsoft: dominates desktop operating systems.
- Rolls-Royce automobiles: luxury motoring.
- Lidl: low-cost retailing through scale and restricted choice.

These businesses became leaders in their fields by relentlessly pursuing just one idea. That is the power of a good idea. But equally, it can be the undoing of a business. Tesco became UK market leader through low cost sustained by huge out-of-town grocery stores. But it has struggled against a pincer attack from even lower-cost rivals such as Lidl and Aldi, which have much narrower ranges (2,000–3,000 lines each versus 30,000–40,000 at Tesco);

at the other end of the market Tesco is being attacked by higher price, quality and service retailers such as Waitrose, which also offer more convenience. Even Microsoft is at risk as mobile computing makes users more comfortable with alternative operating systems such as Android, which are typically free. It is hard to compete against free.

Chapter 3

Crafting your idea: creating the future perfect

Perhaps the worst advice ever given to leaders is 'first things first'. That implies we deal with the here and now. That sounds practical, but in practice it is a recipe for firefighting, dealing with crises and being endlessly reactive to all the noise and chaos of day-to-day management. By working this way, leadership becomes a random walk from today to the future: you react to whatever comes along and then see where you land up. If the wind is blowing north, you head north. When it blows west, you head west.

Today's reality is clearly a constraint and an opportunity: you have to deal with it. But you need to do more than react to events, you have to shape events to your ends.

As a leader, your starting point is to imagine your future perfect. As an exercise, imagine: how do you want your team, your world, your role to look in 3–5 years' time? Do not be constrained by what you have today – work out what you really want. Describe your future perfect in as much detail as possible: what you will be doing, what your team will look like, what you will have achieved and what will be different. If it looks much the same as today, either you are in a dream role, or you are not stretching yourself far enough.

Once you know your future perfect, you can start working back from there. Instead of first things first, start at the end. If you don't know where you are going, you are unlikely to get there.

As you imagine your future perfect, there may be dozens of things you need to do. But out of all of that, there are probably two or three things that really matter. Focus on those – work out how to achieve the big things first, then slowly work into more detail after that. Do not overwhelm yourself with detail from the start.

This future perfect is your lodestar, which tells you what your priorities should be, where you should focus and what sort of team and support you will need. It also tells you what you should do less of, or what you should delegate. By separating out the important from the less important, it becomes a very useful time-management tool.

Your future perfect idea must be simple enough that it can be interpreted and made relevant for shareholders, trustees, staff, suppliers and customers. They all have other things to worry about, such as mortgages, shopping, holidays, bills and the weekend. Your vision probably comes somewhere below buying the cat food. The cat will survive without your vision but will not survive without some food. It takes real effort to make people take notice, let alone take action, as a result of your vision.

> Your future perfect idea must be simple enough that it can be interpreted and made relevant.

The need for a simple direction becomes more important as the world becomes more complicated and change happens at least as fast as ever. In practice, it takes either genius or courage to create simplicity out of complexity.

It's time to look at some effective future perfect ideas in practice. A good future perfect idea gives everyone a clear idea of where they are going, what they are meant to do and what they should not do. Such ideas can come in many shapes and many fashions. Here are three examples:

1   The Red Arrows: the perfect show.

2   Ryanair: the low-cost airline.

3   NASA: first man on the moon.

These are mind-numbingly simple and obvious statements. They do not take long to understand. They provide total focus on what is important. In each case, a simple idea drives the organisation.

The Red Arrows

The Red Arrows are the air display team of the RAF. They have a clear vision – to achieve the perfect air show. They do not try to mark themselves against other air show teams. The only measure of success is perfection.

The search for perfection pervades everything they do, from careful selection of team members to planning of each mission and detailed debriefing of each mission afterwards to see what they need to do better to reach perfection. They have total clarity and focus on what is important to them.

Ryanair

There are many ways for airlines to compete: in-flight service, loyalty schemes, convenient schedules, route network, legroom, on-board entertainment, quality of food and wine, airport lounges, sleeper beds, punctuality, choice of airport, quality of connections.

Michael O'Leary, the founder of Ryanair, has a simple response to all these competitive challenges: low cost, low cost, low cost, low cost, low cost, low cost, low cost, low cost, low cost, low cost, low cost and low cost.

This is very simple, very focused and very effective. Everyone, including the customer, understands what this means for them. Everything flows from the low-cost focus:

- Aircraft: one type to minimise costs.
- Marketing: cut out travel agent, minimise costs.
- Ticketing: electronic confirmation, no costly paper.
- Punctuality: high to maximise fleet usage, minimise costs.
- Airports: secondary airports, low landing fees, quick turnarounds.

As a low-cost carrier, Ryanair has a different market and different model from the flag carriers and is best positioned to survive the shake-out of the low-cost carrier market. In contrast, the staff of flag carriers find themselves confused by serving different markets (budget travellers and premium business travellers) with different messages and different needs. The difference is visible to all: on British Airways you see businesspeople in suits. A suit is rare on Ryanair.

This idea has served Ryanair well for more than 15 years and enabled it to become the largest carrier in Europe, with over 82 million passengers in 2014. But any idea can be challenged: competitors offering more convenient airports and better service, for instance. As a result, Ryanair has taken the radical step of trying to be nicer to its customers. In Michael O'Leary's words: 'It's a newfound experience, I must admit, for me. But if it works this well, I wish I'd been nicer to our customers much earlier.'

> Even the best ideas are not forever. You have to adapt to survive.

Even the best ideas are not forever. You have to adapt to survive.

NASA

In 1962 President Kennedy promised to put a man on the moon within the decade and bring him back alive again. It was a classic future perfect idea: it created a simple, clear and compelling goal which harnessed the efforts of the nation.

To deliver the mission, he created the National Aeronautics and Space Administration (NASA). The idea was compelling and eventually successful, even though at the time no one knew whether it would be possible. The power of the idea can be seen by what has happened to NASA since the moon landings. It has had some successes (Hubble) and some failures (Challenger), but it has lost its original focus and drive. Kennedy's vision was inspired by the need to catch up with Russia (the old Soviet Union) in space. Yuri Gagarin was the first man into space and the USA did not want to give control of space to its cold war enemy.

RUSSIA gives you a simple way of testing the power of your idea:

- **R**elevant. Is your vision relevant to your needs? America faced losing the space race, so Kennedy's vision was highly relevant.

- **U**nique. Could you apply your vision ('be world class') to another company? If so, it is not good. NASA's vision was unique.

- **S**imple. If no one can remember your vision, they will not act on it. More than 50 years later, Kennedy's vision is still powerful and memorable.

- **S**tretching. Leadership is about taking people where they would not have gone by themselves. That means stretching them. NASA's vision was certainly about going where no one had gone before.

- **I**ndividual. Is it clear what each person is meant to do to achieve the vision? NASA's simple vision gave everyone very clear direction about what they were meant to do and where they were meant to focus.

- **A**ctionable. Your vision must be actionable and measurable – it should help staff decide priorities and make clear what they should do and what they should not do.

How does your future perfect idea fare against the RUSSIA test?

Chapter 4

Ideas when you are leading from the middle

I n many ways, leading in the middle of the organisation is far harder than leading from the top. In the middle, you have fewer resources, less control, more bosses and more conflicting priorities than you do at the top. And at the top, it is perhaps easier to see the big picture and set the grand vision. When you are leading from the middle, you cannot chart your own independent course, your big idea has to support the greater good. But this should not stop you making a difference. A couple of examples will illustrate the point.

The facilities manager

The senior partner had made a big speech in which he said the future of the firm depended on much better teamwork. If they were to serve global firms with diverse needs, then all the partners needed to work together to provide a properly integrated service to their clients. This meant that each partner could no longer operate as an independent fiefdom. It was a big idea and it made sense, even if the partners were not sure they really liked the idea of giving up their fiefdoms.

The head of facilities was not at the meeting: he was deemed to be far too unimportant. But he heard about the big idea and wondered what he could do about it. As facilities manager he was responsible for aspects such as catering,

> At the top, it is perhaps easier to see the big picture and set the grand vision.

toilets, property and cleaning. How on earth can a facilities manager help the partners serve their global clients better through improved teamwork?

Eventually, the facilities manager plucked up courage to see the senior partner. He went to the executive suite where the flowers are always fresher and the carpets are always deeper. He entered the vast office of the senior partner, with its pictures and reproduction antiques.

The facilities manager cleared his throat: 'If you really want the partners to work together as a team, the first thing you need to do is get rid of all the offices. They stop your associates talking to each other and stop partners seeing each other. So perhaps you should start by getting rid of the partners' office. As senior partner, you should be the first to go.'

There was a stunned silence. The senior partner had really meant that everyone else needed to change. But he was smart enough to recognise that he had heard the truth. He arranged for the most senior partners in the firm to share an office – it was large and magnificent, but it was a shared office, not a series of private offices. From there, the revolution spread quickly across the firm: offices and cubicles were replaced by open-plan offices, and even hot desks for some. Communication and teamwork became a reality. And the facilities manager had suddenly become someone of stature: he had made a difference with a big idea which helped the firm build its future perfect.

The risk manager

The bank had a near-death experience during the financial crisis and survived only because of a government bailout. After the immediate crisis was resolved, the CEO had to think about how to rebuild a sustainable bank. Following the crisis, the bank had been very internally focused: reducing costs, selling assets, cutting headcount and streamlining operations. The CEO knew that you cannot cut your way to success: he needed to offer a better and brighter future. So he decided that the bank was going to become the most customer-focused bank in the market: it was a big idea, which had huge implications for everyone who worked there.

Well, not quite everyone. The risk department in any bank is widely disliked. They are seen as the people who like to say 'no'; they stop things happening and are always asking for more information, more reports and more detail. They cost the bank money, but earn nothing for it. They are among the least customer-focused people in the bank.

The head of risk realised that this was a great opportunity. If he could make risk more customer focused, he could transform the way it was seen in the bank. So he started by spending a day a month in bank branches to see how the front line really worked. It was eye opening: he saw how risk procedures slowed down decision making, often asked for irrelevant or duplicate information and missed other information that was important. He overhauled the way risk worked to make it properly customer focused, asking for the right information at the right time to enable quick decisions to be made. Quick decisions are often the difference between sealing a deal and losing it.

Both the risk manager and the facilities manager showed how you can turn the CEO's agenda into a big idea for your area. This is like music to the ears of a CEO. CEOs often find they are fighting against management and apathy to make their ideas happen. For instance, the head of a European professional services firm decided she wanted to move from a geographic focus to an industry focus. Naturally, the Italians, Germans, French and British all argued that their markets were unique. But her logic was clear: the only way to develop deep expertise in industries like telecommunications, pharmaceuticals or insurance was to build that expertise across Europe. Fortunately, one or two country heads saw the light – the Dutch head was willing to give up his role to help move to the industry focus. When the new structure was announced, the country heads who had opposed the move found themselves looking for jobs; those who had supported the move suddenly found themselves running pan-European operations.

> CEOs often find they are fighting against management and apathy to make their ideas happen.

When your CEO has a clear agenda, it pays to work out how you can support it rather than sabotage it. Take their idea and convert it into a big idea for your own area. That way, you will make a difference, you will get support from the CEO and you will be noticed.

Chapter 5

Communicating your future perfect idea

So you have your future perfect idea, but how do you communicate it? If you launch into your 200-page PowerPoint presentation, you are not likely to succeed. Inflicting death by bullet point is not a good way to treat your team. Equally, if you stand on your desk and announce 'I have a dream ...', your team may quietly arrange some psychiatric help for you.

Fortunately, you do not need to be a great orator like Pericles, Churchill or Martin Luther King. All you need to be able to do is tell a story, and we can all do that. It should be a simple story, in three parts:

- This is where we are and why we must change.
- This is where we are going and what it means for you.
- This is how we will get there and how you can help us get there.

This is pretty simple stuff. The simpler it is, the better. In today's world we suffer a surfeit of choice. The resulting complexity and confusion are impediments that we cannot afford. A good idea creates clarity and helps people at all levels make better decisions.

CEOs like to read the company newsletter and annual report. There are normally lots of flattering photographs of the CEO looking magisterial behind a desk, looking dynamic at a company site, looking important with a royal or a government minister and looking generous and sociable at a company awards event. Generally, the role of company newsletters is to confirm to the CEO that they are a wonderful person.

> A good idea creates clarity and helps people at all levels make better decisions.

Now think back to when you started work. How often did you read the company newsletter or believe what it said? Sadly, some CEOs still think that a few elegantly written articles, a couple of inspirational emails and a lavishly produced video supported by an equally lavish company conference will build excitement and commitment to the new vision. Think again.

Communicating the vision is a combination of broadband (one-to-many) communication and narrowband (one-to-one) communication.

Communicating the vision in broadband

Successful communication comes down to three elements:

1 One consistent message.
2 Constant repetition.
3 Multiple methods of communicating.

Look back to the successful visions. They could be summarised in one sentence or just a phrase. If you have a clever and complicated vision, throw it out. Make it simple and you have a chance of it being remembered.

> Constant repetition gets the message home.
> Constant repetition gets the message home.
> Constant repetition gets the message home.
> Constant repetition gets the message home.
> Constant repetition gets the message home.

Constant repetition gets the message home.

Constant repetition gets the message home.

Constant repetition gets the message home.

Constant repetition gets the message home.

Constant repetition gets the message home.

Do not try to be subtle. I will confess to being guilty of creating some advertising for Daz (the famous British detergent brand). Over 40 years the basic message has not changed: Daz is great for whiteness. It is not subtle, but at least people seem to remember the message. Even if you have repeated the message many times to the same group, do not assume that you can move on to other messages. Repeat it again.

Finally, use multiple methods of communication. Some are obvious – newsletters, emails, company conferences, meetings, training events, the website and walkabouts all give the chance to hammer home the message. The more you talk about it, the more challenge and feedback you will receive and the better you will become at communicating the message and refining it for each audience.

Celebrate successes and war stories. When you find someone who has done something that embodies the vision you are creating, recognise them and reward them in public.

Communicating the vision in narrowband

Ultimately, leadership is an engagement sport. You cannot lead by remote control. As John le Carré wrote: 'A desk is a dangerous place from which to view the world.' This is as true of leaders as it is of spies.

> You need to create a team and a network of people who have faith in your story.

You need to create a team and a network of people who have faith in your story. Clearly, your top team needs to buy in. If they do not buy in, they need to move on. A team that is playing against itself is unlikely to succeed.

Less obviously, you need to engage a specific network of individuals across your organisation. You need to get the informal grapevine of the organisation working for you. Relying on broadband media to get your message across is not enough.

Newsletters tend to have the style and credibility of *Pravda* in the days of the Soviet Union. You need to get up close and personal with the owners of the grapevine.

Some of this will happen in the natural, semi-random process of meeting different people in different situations. In practice, there are a few individuals who are likely to carry informal influence out of all proportion to their formal position in the organisation. They might run a social club. They might be the crusty old-timer who has seen it all many times before and has watched CEOs come and go with regularity. These people can spread poison, but they can also spread hope. Because they are outside the formal hierarchy they are trusted, and because they have wide networks they are influential. These are the people who feed the grapevine – if they say the new vision makes sense to them, people listen.

One chief executive reviewed the first three years of his tenure and estimated that more than half of his time was spent on communicating his future perfect idea. People do not get it easily. If you have spent six months developing and refining your idea, do not expect anyone else to really understand it in a 45-minute presentation. You have to be persistent and creative about how you communicate.

Bringing cobblers to heel: communicating the service idea

John Timpson owns and runs a chain of 650 shoe repair shops. This is potentially one of the dullest, smallest and most dead-end industries that anyone could inflict on themselves. But he has made his business a success and his employees are proud to be part of his firm. To succeed,

▶

Timpson realised that he was as much in the customer service business as the shoe repair business. Good service meant more custom. 'Good service' is a deceptively simple idea, which drove his entire business. He realised that it was easier to hire good people and train them to repair shoes than to hire grumpy cobblers and train them to be happy and service-focused staff. He realised he needed a revolution.

Timpson trained his area managers to select staff on service aptitude, not technical skills. They listened and they did not get it. They still hired cobblers, albeit slightly less grumpy cobblers. Eventually, Timpson changed the hiring assessment form. All the words went out. In came pictures of 'Mr Men'. Mr Neat, Mr Happy, Mr Prompt, Mr Smart and Mr Reliable all were on one side of the form. Mr Messy, Mr Late, Mr Fib and Mr Lazy pictures were on the other side of the form. The area managers had to circle which of the Mr Men each recruit most resembled. This was not good on diversity. But it worked. Area managers understood it and started to hire the right people. Timpson pulled away from all the traditional cobblers by offering great service from great staff who kept the customers happy and loyal.

Chapter 6

Build your idea into a plan

A James Bond villain is not necessarily the best guide to good management practice, unless you are a megalomaniac who wants world domination. But we will make an exception for Elliot Carver, the mad media mogul who wanted to start World War III to get a good story. Reflecting on his career, he remarked: 'When I was sixteen, I went to work for a newspaper in Hong Kong. It was a rag, but the editor taught me one important lesson. The key to a great story is not who, or what, or when, but why.'

> The key to a great story is also the key to a great plan.

The key to a great story is also the key to a great plan. Just like a journalist, you need to answer the basic questions: what, why, when, who and how. This is what lies behind each question:

- **What?** What is your objective? How will you know when you have succeeded? What will be different as a result of your plan? You should be able to state this goal in one short sentence. A simple goal creates clarity and focus. Having six goals means you will miss some and hit others, and gives your team no real guidance on priorities.

- **Why?** Why is this relevant, and to who? Either you are solving some existing problem, or you are exploring a new opportunity, or you are supporting a broader agenda of top management. Ideally, this will be relevant to leaders at the top and right across the organisation. If they are feeling pain, if they see the need for change, then they will give you the support, people and money you need. If it is your personal challenge, then do not expect much support.

- **When?** Your goal should be time limited: when do you expect to finish? And what are the key milestones on the way? This is where you can draw up a simple critical path that tells you and the team what needs to happen when, and in what order. It is your early warning system to let you know whether you are on track or not.

- **Who?** Who do you need on your team? Whose support do you need in other parts of the business, perhaps to give permissions, give budget, give technical help? You need to build a coalition to make things happen: the bigger the prize, the stronger the coalition needs to be.

- **How?** What are the big risks and issues you need to deal with, and how will you deal with them?

> It is not enough to have an idea, you have to have the discipline to define it clearly and work through the consequences.

All of this is painfully obvious, but what is obvious is often ignored. The result is that a team sets off with great enthusiasm to change things, and then quickly gets lost in a swamp of confusion around priorities and focus. It is not enough to have an idea, you have to have the discipline to define it clearly and work through the consequences.

Know what you want

We went to see the Department for Education. We had a way of improving school performance. We were so confident about our plan that we were prepared to be paid only for the results we achieved. In other words, if results did not improve, we would be paid nothing. This was a good deal for the taxpayer: the taxpayer risked no money at all. It had to be an easy sale.

We saw various officials, who are always cautious about any new idea. So it was probably a mistake when I said that we really needed only two things from them: they had to tell us what success looked like from their perspective, and how much they valued it. That way, they could set the goals and decide how much to pay for the results.

There was a stunned silence. After decades of running the nation's education, it soon became clear that they did not know how to define success, let alone how much to value it. They knew exam results counted, but argued about which subjects counted the most; they knew that things like sport, music, drama and giving the child a rounded experience counted; they also knew that preparing students for the world of work mattered, which means dealing with people, learning responsibility and acquiring practical skills. But they had no idea how to create clear goals out of this.

This helps explain the challenge of deciding education policy. When you don't know what success looks like, any idea can be a good idea or a bad idea depending on how you are feeling that day.

Chapter 7

Sell your idea

There are three keys to selling your idea:

1 Listen.
2 Prepare and question.
3 Know your idea.

Listen

We all have great ideas, especially after a few drinks with our friends. In the cold light of day, most ideas vanish as fast as a vampire fleeing the dawn. The first test of any idea is whether anyone else believes in it and is ready to back it. So how do you build your coalition of support?

First, you need the secret of all great leaders and great sales people: you need two ears and one mouth. And you need to use them in that proportion. Listen at least twice as much as you talk. Persuasion is not about having a great pitch, it is about knowing what other people want and what they think. If you don't know what they want, you cannot influence them. See the world through their eyes: what are their goals and priorities, what are the problems they face, how much risk will they take, what is their personal agenda? Knowledge is power: acquire it, use it.

Listening is not just about acquiring knowledge, it is also about building trust. We live in a world where we find it hard to have our voice heard – it is easy

> Knowledge is power: acquire it, use it.

to feel ignored and overlooked. So how do you feel when someone takes the time and trouble to seek your views and to listen to you? The normal reaction is to feel some combination of gratitude, pleasure and relief. It is then normal to reciprocate – we think more highly of people who appear to think highly of us.

Listen to persuade

The partners of the professional services firm were all very bright. Well, most of them. Among the bright sparks there was one who shone as brightly as a small, flickering candle. She did not really fit in. She had no presence, and spoke awkwardly. But clients loved her, which was irritating to all the bright spark partners who would often find themselves arguing with clients to get their way.

One day I saw her with a client at 10am. She appeared to be listening intently. At 2pm, I passed by again and she was still there, still listening. At 6pm the client emerged, wreathed in smiles. The client told me that he had just persuaded our partner to help his firm on a three-year change programme. Finally, he could see a way through his challenges.

I was stunned. The partner had just sold three years of work and the client saw it as a personal triumph. I asked how she did it. 'I just let them empty out their hearts and minds. Only when they have emptied themselves are they ready to be filled with my thoughts. Of course, by that point I can tailor my thoughts to exactly what they want. It's easy if you listen.'

Prepare and question

The art of listening is also the art of asking good questions. It is harder to ask good questions than to make a big speech. With a speech, you are in control and you say what you want. With a conversation, you are no longer in full control. The person you are talking to might surprise you with new information, ideas or insights. This means that an important conversation requires more preparation than an important presentation.

A good discipline is to work out in advance what are the five questions you least want the other person to ask and what are the five issues you would least like them to raise. Those are the questions and issues you are most likely to have to deal with. If you are surprised by the way the conversation goes, you probably have not done your preparation properly.

Good questions are normally open questions. Open questions encourage a full response. A closed question is one that allows a yes/no answer. The examples below will make the point.

Open questions	Closed questions
What are your main goals this year?	Are you on track to hit budget?
What do you like about this new idea?	Do you like this idea?
How can we make this affordable?	Do we have enough budget for this?
How can we get the support of the CEO?	Does the CEO support this?

Closed questions are dangerous. They carry the risk of a negative response. Even a positive response yields little information for you. Once you have a negative response, you are into a conflict where you have to persuade the other person that you are right and they are wrong. It is a lose–lose debate. Open questions invite dialogue and encourage problem solving together.

Know your idea

Of course, you know what your idea is. But the real test is whether you know why anyone else would want to act on your idea. The great risk is that you fall in love with your idea and are blind to its flaws. Be objective. See what the idea looks like from someone else's point of view. You do not really know your idea until you know how others will judge it.

As CEO you may be enthusiastic about a brave new world where you create a lean and mean organisation: that means a buzz word fest of delayering, outsourcing, offshoring, best shoring, right sizing and process simplification. In other words, you want to fire lots of staff.

Not surprisingly, your staff may be less enthusiastic about this brave new world. Even after you have gone through the bloodletting, the survivors are likely to feel bruised, anxious and not very confident about their future. If you are to secure high performance from them, you need to paint a picture that reaches beyond firing people and gives them hope of a better future.

> As CEO you may be enthusiastic about a brave new world where you create a lean and mean organisation.

At a less dramatic level, you may have a great idea for improving the work of your department. But if that means you need the help and cooperation of other departments, do not be surprised if you are met by a wall of apathy. Other departments have other needs and are probably already fully stretched – the last thing they need is to do more work to help someone else and perhaps risk messing up their own work.

As you evaluate your idea, there are two questions you should ask yourself:

1 What's the problem?
2 What's the prize?

What is the problem you are solving and whose problem is it? A good problem to solve is one where there is a lot of pain. No one likes pain. This is what CEOs occasionally call the 'burning platform'. If there is a fire, people want to put it out. CEOs are not above creating a crisis, which normally runs along the lines of: 'If we don't change now we will be out of business because of those nasty competitors or foreigners.' Faced with the prospect of losing our job, most of us are prepared to change the way we work.

If no one is feeling any pain, then you may have a good idea but you will find it hard to create a sense of urgency. Your idea will be a 'nice to have' rather than a 'must have' idea.

The second question is: 'What's the prize?' The bigger the prize, the harder people will work for it, the more support you will get and the more the organisation will commit to making it happen. The prize can be qualitative, quantitative (non-financial) or financial. The table shows the difference.

Qualitative	Quantitative (non-financial)	Financial
We will improve staff morale	Staff attrition will drop from 23% to 10% annually	We will save £3 million annually on selection and hiring costs
We will increase customer satisfaction	We will reduce delivery lead times by 40%	We will generate another £25 million in sales and £5 million in contribution annually

Typically, most organisations find the financial prize the most compelling. Every time someone raises a problem or an issue, you can wave the financial prize in front of them: 'Do you really want to forgo £5 million annual contribution because of that issue?' No executive wants to be seen as the person who stopped the firm making another £5 million a year. Objections tend to melt away in the face of a big prize. In contrast, a vague promise to 'increase customer satisfaction' will not get far. Know your idea well enough so that you can size the prize.

Naturally, the prize needs to be credible. If you think you can make another £5 million a year by reducing delivery lead times, then you need your idea to be validated by the right people. Marketing and sales need to agree that reduced lead times lead to more customers; operations need to agree that the reduced delivery lead times are viable; finance needs to agree that your numbers add up. When validating your proposal, do not ask the experts to approve the whole plan – you will be held hostage by too many vested interests. Simply ask each expert to validate the assumptions that are relevant to their part of the organisation. Build your case one brick at a time.

Chapter 8

Dealing with strategy

As a leader, at some point you have to deal with formal strategy. The first challenge is to know what strategy is. The word has become debased. It now means anything that the speaker thinks is important, as in a strategic review, a strategic investment, a strategic campaign. Even strategists disagree about the nature of strategy. In practice, there are two approaches to strategy that are worth knowing about: the classical approach and the modern approach.

> The first challenge is to know what strategy is.

Classical strategy

Corporate strategy helps a large business decide where it should focus its efforts and whether it is in the right markets. This is the land of portfolio analysis: look at the organisation as a portfolio of separate businesses and assess their relative attractiveness. This can be done on the basis of predicted cash flows based on market growth and market share relative to competition (which forms the basis of the BCG growth share matrix) or on the basis of market attractiveness and competitive position (the GE grid).

The basic theory of portfolio analysis is laid out in Figure 8.1.

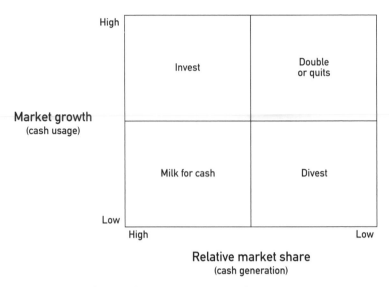

Figure 8.1 Portfolio analysis: the BCG growth share matrix
Source: Adapted from The BCG Portfolio Matrix from the Product Portfolio Matrix, © 1970, The Boston Consulting Group (BCG). Reproduced with permission.

But theory rarely survives first contact with reality, at least on planet business. The world is not as neat as a business school case implies, and there is never a professor on hand to tell you the correct answer. As the text box story shows, you should use analytical tools as an aid to judgement, not as a substitute for judgement.

> Theory rarely survives first contact with reality.

Tools versus thinking

I was very pleased. I had been asked to recommend to a client board what they should do with their portfolio of food businesses. I duly produced endless two-by-two grids. I then got sophisticated and produced some three-by-three grids, some of which I even coloured in.

It was not as easy as at business school. First, it was not clear what defined a business. Is milling wheat really separate from baking? Is bread really one business, or lots of businesses, ranging from the mass-produced white sliced to artisan croissants? And all the answers seemed to come out roughly in the middle of every grid, which meant that I could justify just about anything, except my fees.

Eventually I was able to tease out a story. Milk the mature milling and baking businesses for cash, invest heavily in a South East Asian restaurant chain and sell off some mature cake brands. The answers were fully supported by the grids, like the BCG matrix above, which I had produced.

The partner in charge had not seemed interested in my work. He never even looked at it. As we drove to the client, he quizzed me about my work. When he got up to present to the board, he made exactly the opposite recommendations from my conclusions: invest heavily in milling and baking, sell the South East Asian restaurant chain and invest in the cake brands.

After I had dragged my jaw off the ground, I asked him what he was doing. 'Easy,' he said. 'Everyone in the industry is doing the same dumb portfolio analysis. So they all want to get out of milling and baking. Our client is really good at that. They can pick up assets very cheap with everyone wanting to sell, turn them around and make a fortune. The opposite is true of South East Asian restaurants, so we can sell that for a huge premium and reinvest the proceeds in milling and baking.'

The company went on to thrive with this new strategy, and I had learned a valuable lesson that analysis should be an aid to judgement, not a substitute for judgement.

These analytical tools have a reason to exist. In the case of the BCG matrix and the GE grid, they point to the fundamental need to know where your cash comes from and where it goes to. They also highlight the need to know how strong your business really is.

This is the basis of Michael Porter's five forces analysis. Ideally, you want a business where:

- there is limited direct competition
- there are no easy substitutes
- new entrants are unlikely: there are high barriers to success
- there is limited buyer power
- there is limited supplier power.

A quick comparison will make the point. What are the prospects for Microsoft's business and for my business if I decide to set up a burger palace on the local high street?

	Microsoft	Jo's Burger Palace
Direct competition	Very limited historically – but may be emerging	McDonald's is nearby, plus two other burger joints
Substitutes	A substitute for an operating system? A quill pen?	There are also a pizza parlour and four ethnic restaurants nearby
New entrants	Very high barriers to entry: embedded client base that faces high switching costs and risks	Low rents mean anyone can set up a new restaurant here
Buyer power	Weak: hard for buyers to switch	Clients can walk straight past me, and they do
Supplier power	Minimal: low dependency on any suppliers	I am part of a franchise, so I am at the mercy of my supplier (the franchisor)

A quick look at this would show that I am unlikely to make a fortune from my palace, but Microsoft could make a fortune even if it occasionally produces mediocre software, such as Vista and Windows 8.0. But even here, use judgement. Even if there is tough competition, you can succeed if you have a good idea – in this context a good idea is one that differentiates you from the competition and offers the customers something they want at a price they can afford.

Two burger joints thrive near a successful McDonald's on my local high street. One is an upmarket chain that offers 'proper' burgers. The other is owned by Bill Wyman of the Rolling Stones and is full of his memorabilia. Being Bill Wyman does give you a unique selling proposition that the rest of us will always lack. Analysis may tell you that you will have a hard job succeeding; if you have a good idea, that will let you succeed. A strong idea beats dull analysis every time.

> A strong idea beats dull analysis every time.

These analytical tools can help you test your idea. The great big lie behind these tools is that their creators imply that the tools are both predictive and prescriptive: they predict what will happen and prescribe what you should do about it. It is a very Newtonian world of action and reaction. But we have seen that once everyone uses the same tools, they auto-destruct: because everyone follows the same strategy, the strategies cancel each other out.

Modern strategy

There has been a revolt against the classical world of Porter and endless grids. The revolt was led by CK Prahalad and continued by his acolytes such as Gary Hamel and Chan Kim. This is the world of Strategic Intent, Core Competence and Blue Oceans. These are all wonderful marketing labels that have taken the business world by storm over the last 20 years. Inevitably, they have been grossly misunderstood. For instance, core competence has come to mean anything that we think we might be faintly competent at doing.

We will call the Prahalad school 'modern' strategy simply to differentiate it from the classical approach of Porter *et al*. Modern strategy puts a premium on creativity and discovery rather than on analysis to find the answer. It is well suited to an era of disruptive innovation. Ten years ago, social networking meant going to parties or having coffee with someone. No one had heard of Facebook and no one knew (apart from Mark Zuckerberg) that they needed it. Now, it has become a central part of many people's social lives. Equally, we did not know that we would need Shazam to tell us what music we were listening to, Spotify to stream our favourite music to us, or that we really needed tablet computers with us all day. No amount of analysis using classical strategy tools would have helped us establish Facebook, Shazam or Spotify. If anything, analysis would have told us to avoid these adventures – the big music publishers such as EMI and Universal looked overwhelmingly powerful in the music space; Dell and HP looked overwhelmingly powerful in computers and traditional analysis would not have led Samsung to enter that market. But it is Samsung, not HP or Dell, that has succeeded in tablets, alongside Apple.

So how can you be creative and come up with a great idea? Here are five ways.

Copy someone else

Many brilliant businesses are built by copying someone else. Ryanair is Europe's largest carrier and started off as a direct copy of Southwest Airlines, which had pioneered the low-cost, no-frills approach to flying. Teach First, which is the UK's largest graduate recruiter, was inspired by Teach for America. The iPad became a huge success from launch in 2010, but had been preceded by less successful efforts from AT&T (1991) and Compaq (1993).

Solve a customer problem

If you are irritated or annoyed by something, you can remain irritated and annoyed if you want. Or you can solve the problem and make a fortune. Shazam solved the problem we all occasionally have when we hear some great music and do not know what it is. Shazam provides the solution. Similarly, James Dyson was frustrated by vacuum cleaners that did not clean well, especially when their dust bags started to fill up. After 5,127 prototypes, he eventually found a solution which was good enough that he could take on the might of Hoover and the other dominant vacuum producers.

Spend a day in the life of your customer

This is the quickest way to find out how to make a difference. If airline crews had to suffer the same security, check-in, passport and luggage delays as their passengers, such airport hassles would soon become history. One water company was convinced that it offered great customer service and it had the surveys to show it. Then I showed the staff a video of an elderly customer in tears over a flood they had caused and were not sorting out. See the world through your customer's eyes, not through the warped lens of customer research.

Keep trying

The difference between success and failure is persistence. The more you keep trying, the more you learn about what works and what does not work. We all now know that paid search is the key to success for any search engine, and Google has built a fortune from that. But it was not obvious in the beginning. During the dot.com boom, Yahoo!, Magellan, Lycos, Infoseek and

> The difference between success and failure is persistence.

Excite were all vying for prominence. The market was testing out lots of different approaches. Constant testing produced one winner: Google, now copied by Baidu in China.

Analyse your way to insight

Chan Kim of INSEAD, in Blue Ocean Strategy, offers a way to come up with innovative insight. The premise is simple: draw a value curve of what your customers want and what your competitors offer, then find out where the opportunity lies. A simple example will make the point.

Simplified value curve for a hotel

	What customers want	Typical hotels
A good bed and pillow	✓✓✓✓✓	✓✓✓
A quiet room	✓✓✓✓✓	✓✓✓
A good cafe	✓✓	✓✓✓
Nice reception area and helpful receptionists	✓	✓✓✓✓✓
A health club	✓	✓✓✓✓

This simplified analysis shows that you have an opportunity to change the rules of the game. Invest more in the basics: a good bed and a quiet room so guests can sleep. Avoid spending on things your customers do not value, such as a health club. This is the formula that is now being adopted by budget hotels worldwide.

Modern strategy offers hope to anyone with a great idea. But a large firm with huge resources is no defence against a great idea with a great team. In other words, the IPA agenda (Idea, People, Action) does not respect power or privilege. If you have IPA, you can succeed. That is experience, not hype.

Strong incumbents being challenged

Legacy firms	Challenger firms
BA, Lufthansa	Ryanair, easyJet
Hoover	Dyson
Kodak cameras	Panasonic
Dell, HP	Samsung, Apple
BBC	Sky

In each case in the table, the incumbents appeared to hold all the aces: they had money, market share and skills. The challengers were weak, and any rational analysis would have told them not to take on the giants in a fight – David would not have been advised to tackle Goliath. But in each case, they changed the rules of the game. When the rules change, the incumbents are stuck. If they stick to their existing formula, they let the challengers grow. If they change their formula, they abandon their existing franchise. For instance, if you were BA and looking at the rise of Ryanair, what would you do? In practice, incumbents tend to stick to their tried and tested formula, and the incumbents find their 'Blue Ocean': an uncontested part of the market where they can grow fast.

Bringing modern and classical strategy together

Modern and classical strategy offer you two very different ways of thinking about your business. Both have their value. Typically, modern strategy is most useful for new and disruptive firms, or mature firms that want to break out of their old way of doing things, perhaps to confront new upstarts that are challenging them.

If you use classical strategy, do not check your brain out while doing the analysis. Use the analysis as a starting point, not an end point, for your strategic discussion. If you go down the modern route, do not fall in love with your idea and grow blind to its faults. For every success that comes from modern strategy, there are a thousand failures, people who thought they had a great idea but are still stuck in their attic or garage waiting for the world to discover their brilliance.

> Do not fall in love with your idea and grow blind to its faults.

Chapter 9

Strategy and the art of unfair competition

You will hear much talk about competitive advantage. When an executive talks about their competitive advantage, sell the stock. If you invest, then invest in firms that have a thoroughly unfair source of competitive advantage. An unfair advantage is one that earns a very high return and is hard for competition to shift. Every firm needs a few products or businesses like that. You need to be earning far in excess of your cost of capital in a few areas. These excess returns will help pay for all your investments in the future, for operational and strategic mistakes, and for all those businesses that are still struggling to make the return you want. We live in a world where customers want more for less, the taxman always wants a slightly bigger cut, staff want to be paid more, the competition is cutting prices, innovating and raising quality, and crises and disasters happen on a regular basis. This is a world in which profits can vanish fast. 'Competitive advantage' is a weak defence against such challenges – you want such an unfair source of advantage that regulators and politicians start to take notice.

> Ultimately you want an idea that builds you a source of unfair advantage.

From a strategy perspective, ultimately you want an idea that builds you a source of unfair advantage. Here are some examples of 'unfair' competitive advantage that are highly profitable:

- Have a licence to drill oil in a low-cost oil field (ExxonMobil, Petrobras, Shell).
- Be in the best location on the high street (McDonald's, Starbucks).
- Own copyright, trademarks or patents (Disney and Dyson).
- Be the first to move into a new market that is a natural monopoly (Microsoft for operating systems; Google for paid search; SWIFT for high-value interbank payments).
- Build a powerful brand (P&G, Nike, etc.).
- Own a unique resource (Heathrow landing slots for BA).

These are all sources of great and 'unfair' advantage which could allow the incumbents to be relatively inefficient and still be very profitable. You can decide how many of the named firms fit that description.

In theory, we might all subscribe to the idea that competition is good. From the point of view of society and the development of the economy, competition is good. From the point of view of our own survival, competition is not so good. The problem with a fair fight is that you might lose it. Weight the dice in your favour where you legally can.

Chapter 10

How to evaluate your idea

H ow do you know if your strategic idea is a good idea? You may not have the time or resources to do a full strategic analysis. But you need to respond to all the challenges you are likely to receive from bosses, peers, investors and other interested parties. Be ready to answer the questions before they are asked: challenge yourself before you are challenged.

The challenges you should expect, and set yourself, come in four main flavours, which overlap:

1 Financial.
2 Customer.
3 Competition.
4 Product/operations.

Financial

You will probably have created a financial spreadsheet which shows an attractive number in the bottom right-hand corner. It will be widely disbelieved because most such spreadsheets are built up from the bottom right-hand corner – executives find the magic number people want to see and then construct the spreadsheet to achieve that result. You will not be tested directly on the numbers. You will be tested on the assumptions behind the numbers:

- Have you estimated the right market size, market growth and market share?
- Is your pricing realistic, especially after the competition reacts?
- Do your costs match up against relevant benchmarks?
- Are the size and timing of your cash flows realistic, or will you need more investment?

These are simple, basic tests. Only when your idea has passed these tests should you delve deeper into detail. If you come up with a plan that only just meets the required financial return, expect a hard time. Spreadsheets are always rosier than reality. By the time competition, customers and the unexpected have undermined your projections, your financial return will start to look sickly. The best ideas will beat financial hurdles by a large margin.

Customer

Most great strategies start with an insight about the customer. Be precise when you talk about 'the customer'. Your customer is not the same as the market. If you segment the market well, you may find a niche where you can thrive. For instance, when I took Zest toilet soap to market, market research showed that it was not much liked by the market as a whole. But there was a zealous 10% of the market that loved it and would pay a premium for its distinctive look and fragrance. That is all we needed to succeed.

> If you segment the market well, you may find a niche where you can thrive.

More often you might segment your market by price: premium versus budget. The questions you ask should include:

- Does this answer a real customer need? Are they prepared to pay for it?
- What is the value proposition and how can you communicate it?

- How can you reach your customers: sales channels, distribution channels, media and messaging channels?

- Do your customers form a distinctive niche or segment which you can target?

The best way to test this is to talk to potential customers. Even if you do not have the full product or service to show them, you should be able to describe your offer in a way that gets a reaction. Read reactions carefully: people tend to be polite, so a neutral reaction is negative. When your potential customers start showing enthusiasm for your idea, then you have an idea that might work. The enthusiasts will describe why they like the idea in a way that will allow you to frame your value proposition/message to them credibly and persuasively.

Competition

The competition is often a mystery. Even if we know who they are, it is hard to predict what they will do. It is easy to over-estimate or to under-estimate their threat. If you over-estimate their threat, you may simply give up. If you under-estimate them, you will suffer badly. You have to ask the right questions and answer them as best you can. Find someone who knows the market, or perhaps used to work at a rival, to help you gain insight and come up with plausible answers.

Useful questions to ask include:

- How easy is it for competitors to copy your idea? Do you have any barriers to entry (patents, exclusive rights, strong brand, embedded customers, etc.)?

- What are the alternative products/services to your idea? How attractive are they, at what price?

- How do rival offerings stack up in terms of price and value for the customer segment you want to serve?

- How will competition likely react to your idea: pricing, product, promotions, etc.?

Product/operations

This is your final reality check. Can you actually deliver your product, service or idea at the right cost, time and place? Have you got the team that will ensure success, or are you battling to find the right talent? Typically, venture capitalists back the person as much as they back the idea. The same is true within a firm – great managers are backed more readily than great ideas. This means that you need to line up the best team and ensure you have support and

> Venture capitalists back the person as much as they back the idea.

backing from influential people within or beyond the firm. Use the power of endorsement to your advantage and borrow credibility from influencers where you need to.

Part 2

People: make your network work

Introduction

Much of the leadership industry is based on the idea of the leader as a hero. Fame-hungry CEOs write their self-serving autobiographies. The speaking circuit is full of individuals sharing their inspirational stories. You can find endless books on the great leader heroes of history. This is misleading and unhelpful. It is unhelpful because most of us are not heroic and never will be. Even if Genghis Khan and Nelson Mandela are the right role models, we will struggle to copy them. Fortunately, we do not need to copy them and we do not need to be heroes.

The best leaders do not even try to do it all themselves, not even Genghis Khan or Nelson Mandela. They surround themselves with great people. The best leaders have the best teams. This then raises the obvious question about what leaders really do: if they have a great team, then what is the point of the leader? This is a simple question that even CEOs often struggle to answer – they know what their title is (CEO) but they do not always know what their role should be.

This section of the book looks at how you can build and lead the team that will convert your idea into reality. The art of building and leading your team includes picking, recruiting, coaching and motivating your team and managing their performance. But your team is not just your direct reports, it also includes a wider network of peers that you rely on but do not control. You have to learn how to influence without power. This is most acute when it comes to managing your boss. Most management theory is devoted to managing teams, but most managers worry more about managing their boss. You will also have to manage awkward people and have difficult conversations occasionally, including the unenviable task of firing people or moving them on.

If you have built a truly great team that does everything you want, you are left with a surprising challenge: what is your own role? If the team is that great, is there anything left for you to do? That is not a riddle you want to leave to the end. Answer that question first and you will be clear about what you need to do and what sort of team you need to build. So this part of the book will start by helping you solve this riddle.

Chapter 11

Find your role

The more senior you become, the more ambiguous your role becomes. If you are a junior sales person it is clear what you have to do. You will have clear sales targets that you have to meet. As you move up into management, fog slowly descends. As a manager you will have multiple goals. It becomes clear that you cannot deliver them all by yourself. This means you have to build a team to make things happen for you. But if you have a great team that delivers the results for you, how do you add any value: what is the point of your job?

As an example, we will use Ronald Reagan. By repute he did not work hard, not at least by the standards of most presidents who are in a very demanding role. He found plenty of time for golf. So how can you run the most powerful country on the planet, win the cold war, introduce Reaganomics, negotiate a nuclear arms reduction treaty and still have time for golf?

Reagan was able to do this because he was clear about what his role was. You may or may not approve of Reagan and his legacy, but he succeeded in the narrow sense of achieving roughly what he set out to achieve. That is more than many leaders, presidents or CEOs achieve. He focused on the IPA agenda of leadership:

- Idea: he had a clear idea of what he wanted to achieve: Reaganomics and rolling back the Communist threat.
- People: he built a team around him that could deliver his idea.

- Action: he was clear about his personal role. He was the great speaker who could create hope and optimism, and persuade Congress to support his agenda.

As a leader you need to know where you add value to your team, where you make a difference. If someone in your team can do what you are doing, let them do it. Don't work beneath your role: you don't have the time and you cost too much. This means moving out of your comfort zone of working with familiar challenges.

> **As a leader you need to know where you add value to your team, where you make a difference.**

If you are leading in the middle of the organisation, you may wonder whether your role is the same as that of the President of the United States. Broadly speaking, it is the same:

- Idea: know what you want to achieve.
- People: build and manage the team to deliver your idea.
- Action: create the conditions in which your team can thrive.

Once you know what you have to do, then you can decide what you need the rest of the team to do. As a leader, one of your key roles is to create the conditions in which your team can succeed. That means picking the right team, securing the right budget and resources, ensuring top management support your agenda, running political interference where necessary, dividing up and delegating tasks, and managing performance. These are things that only you as the leader can do – more or less everything else, your team can do for you.

In this section we will explore how you can succeed through other people. In the next section, we will explore how you can drive to action.

Chapter 12

Attract the right team

T he right team is a dream team. It will turn mountains into molehills, it will turn crises into opportunities and surprises may even turn out to be pleasant. However, if you settle for the 'B' team, you will struggle. Every setback will be a crisis; you will hear more excuses than you want; you will waste time settling disputes within the team; and you will find yourself losing sleep every time a deadline looms. At this point you may quietly curse your team. But you should curse yourself – attracting the right team is one of the most important tasks that any leader undertakes. The quality of your team sets the limit to what you can achieve.

In practice, there are plenty of reasons why you may find yourself with the 'B' team, not the 'A' team. The team you inherit will be only as good as the leader you succeed. If you are lucky, you will be following in the footsteps of a great leader and

> The team you inherit will be only as good as the leader you succeed.

you will inherit a great team. But instead of relying on the luck of the lottery, you can stack the odds in your favour by making sure you attract the right team.

First, you need to know what the 'right' team looks like. The right team will be a mix of three characteristics:

1 Right skills.
2 Right style.
3 Right values.

Normally, great focus is put on finding the right skills. This is dangerous. As one CEO put it: 'I find I hire most people for their skills, and fire most for their (poor) values.' Think about the people who cause the greatest challenges where you work. The chances are that they do not have a problem with their skills, they have a problem with their values. Here is what you need to look for in each of the three characteristics.

Right skills

Skills are important, and there is much talk of the 'war for talent'. Clearly, there are some deeply technical and specialist skills for which you have to pay a premium. Anyone who has had to hire a law firm to deal with major litigation will understand just how expensive good technical talent can be. So if you need technical talent, find the best and be ready to pay for it.

But most other skills are becoming a commodity. You can find plenty of people with different IT or accounting skills, and increasingly these are skills that can be outsourced or offshored. Other skills can be learned by team members in the course of their work.

Unless you are in a situation where you need a specialist skill set that is in high demand, the chances are that you will have a choice between people with roughly comparable skill sets. So you need a way of choosing between them.

The first, obvious, screen is to see what people have achieved with their skills. This leads to some equally obvious bear traps. First, people tend to puff up their achievements. In recruiting graduates, I find they have all achieved extraordinary things – each one claims to have volunteered, run marathons, started societies and built their own businesses. On the back of this, they want to become a trainee, even though they appear to be well on the way to becoming millionaires in their own right. Check facts, take references.

The second challenge with looking at achievements is that firms routinely value external experience above internal: it is the mirror image of employees believing that the grass is greener elsewhere. Remember that it is greenest where it rains the most. In practice, external hires are risky. You do not really know what they have achieved or why they want to move. All new hires suffer a transition dip because they no longer have the networks of informal influence that made them effective in their last role. And even if they do work through the transition, many struggle to adapt to a new culture. The more senior the hire is (with the exception of the CEO), the greater these challenges are. At least if you look for talent within your own organisation, you are likely to know what the person has really achieved, they will still have their networks of influence and they will understand the culture.

> Remember that it is greenest where it rains the most.

The third challenge with hiring externally is to understand how someone has achieved their successes. There is a delicate balance here: if they lead the success, then are they really a team player or a one-man band? If they were a team member, then can they really lead? It is, potentially, a catch-22 situation where the candidate cannot win.

Right style

Most leaders understand that you need a mix of skills to succeed. If the executive committee of a large firm was made up purely of accountants, or IT people or just sales people, it would be easy to spot that it was unbalanced and unlikely to work well.

When it comes to skills, leaders see the need for balance and mix. When it comes to styles, many leaders avoid balance and mix – they want uniformity and conformity. This is not about the traditional take on diversity – balancing your team in terms of gender, age, race, ethnicity and perhaps left handers and right handers is worthy but misses the point. There are plenty of firms out there that trumpet their diversity credentials and then in the same breath trumpet the fact that they are a 'one-firm firm' all over the world, with the same values. In other words, their diversity is skin deep. You can be any age, race, colour or religion, but you must sign up to a single set of values, beliefs and ways of doing things.

Within a team, leaders make the same mistake. It is tempting to hire people like yourself – at least you have some idea how to work with people like yourself. For example, see what happens when you select your team on two simple trade-offs: extravert versus introvert; detail focus versus big picture. Here is what your team will be like if they all share the same style of trade-off:

● Team of introverts: the room will echo to the sound of silence.

● Team full of extraverts: more chaos than a chimpanzees' tea party.

● Team of big-picture people: great debates, no action.

● Team of detail people: everyone diligently marching in the wrong direction.

Here are some other style trade-offs for you to think about as you build your team:

● task focused versus people focused

● controlling versus empowering

● risk taking versus risk averse

● individualistic versus team player

● flexible versus structured.

A good starting point is to think about your own style on these trade-offs and others that are important to you. Then consider whether the rest of the team should be the same as you or whether you need some balance.

Inevitably, it is harder to work with people who are not like yourself. It takes time to understand each other. But it is also more productive. You bring different perspectives and different strengths into the team, and you may even learn from each other about different ways of making things happen.

There is no single formula for the 'right' balance of a team – you have to make that judgement. This is one of the reasons that leadership is an art which a robot will find hard to replicate.

Right values

You can teach skills, you cannot teach values. In principle, you will succeed more often if you hire to values, not to skills. A good example came from the insurance company MetLife, which was hiring more than 5,000 people a year to become sales people. Over 80% would leave within four years, which was a poor return on the $30,000 cost of hiring and training each sales person. The company then started adding an optimism test to its regular screening. It found that the most optimistic candidates outsold their peers by 88%. Even the optimists who failed the regular screening (but were hired to test the power of optimism) outsold pessimists who passed the regular screening by 57%. MetLife duly changed its hiring practices. These results have been replicated in real estate, autos, office products and banking.

> You can teach skills, you cannot teach values.

In terms of style, you can afford to be non-judgemental: different styles work in different situations. In terms of values, you should be judgemental. There are good values and there are toxic values. Try the following contrasts:

- industrious or idle
- honest or dishonest
- optimistic or pessimistic

- helpful or selfish
- open or devious
- reliable or sloppy.

We have all had to work with bosses and colleagues who had the wrong values. It is not worth it. Be clear about the values you want and those you want to avoid. Then hire to your desired values.

> Be clear about the values you want and those you want to avoid.

Once you know who you want to hire, you have to find a way of hiring them. This is easier said than done. If you are hiring the right people, the chances are that they are in high demand. Their existing boss will not want to lose them, and they will have plenty of options open to them. So why on earth would they choose to come and work with you?

When you are recruiting, you are selling: you are selling a role, and you are selling yourself. As we have already seen, the starting point for persuading is listening. If in doubt, let people talk about their favourite subject: themselves. The sweetest sound in the world is their own voice. Indulge them, however painful it may be. By listening to them, you can start to understand what drives them, what they want as the next steps in their career, what is frustrating them now, what they like and dislike. This can be a major investment of time and effort. But it is an investment that yields significant returns for you as a boss. They are giving the sales pitch you need to make. Once you understand them, you can present the role in the way they want to hear. And you can also present yourself in the way that they want.

The major bear trap at this point is to get locked into negotiations on salary. If the candidate is primarily driven by money, you may want to ask whether they have the values you want. You may also ask whether they have good judgement. I have had graduates argue over 5–10% on their starting salary. I would be more impressed if they argued about how they could increase their salary tenfold – that is a discussion about what sort of career they want, and what they need to learn and do in order to succeed. Even in mid-career, executives will have another 20 years ahead of them – helping them have a rewarding job in the short term and a successful career in the long term should be more important than doing a special deal on starting salary. Remember that any such special deal normally leaks into the public domain, leading to demands for special deals from all the other team members. Chaos and resentment ensue.

Chapter 13

Motivate your team: theory

C hurchill described Russia as a 'riddle, wrapped in a mystery, inside an enigma'. He may as well have been describing human nature. The collective efforts of tens of thousands of shrinks over the last 100 years have not made people happier or more motivated. They have shown that we are all more messed up than we ever thought. Stress, low self-esteem, depression and other mental dysfunctions are at epidemic levels.

All the leader has to do is to solve the riddle wrapped in the mystery inside the enigma. The leader has to succeed where all the shrinks have failed – your riddle is to find a way of motivating your team. This is your key to unlocking the potential of your team and achieving high performance. A demotivated team is no use to you at all.

To solve this we will look at three approaches:

1 Three practical theories of motivation.
2 How leaders apply the theory in practice.
3 Motivation and moments of truth.

Before we embark on the journey in search of motivation, it is worth being clear about what motivation is and what it is not. It helps if we are searching for the right thing.

Motivation is not inspiration. There is too much talk about inspirational leaders. There are some inspirational leaders out there, but most of us are not natural inspirers. We can do many basic things well that will motivate people. We may even inspire people if we do the basics well enough. But if we set off in search of inspiration we are likely to find ourselves in the land of men in white suits waving their arms on stages, whipping massed audiences into a frenzy of excitement. They can sell inspiration, insurance or religion with equal vigour. Sustaining motivation for the weeks, months and years that follow the speech is a different art form.

> Sustaining motivation for the weeks, months and years that follow is a different art form.

Practical theories of motivation: part one

Let's start with a simple choice. Let us assume that you are a budding leader who likes work, you are committed to it, you live to work and to lead, and you are deeply involved in your business. Look around you, not just at your peers but also at people at all levels of your organisation. If they are all like you in their attitude to your organisation, pick Y. If you think people fundamentally dislike work, are lazy, work to live and feel alienated from work, pick X.

Obviously, how you motivate people will depend on whether you think they are X-types or Y-types. It is possible that you are surrounded by a mixture of the two.

Let's start with the X-types. In a perfect world, you would be able to convert them into happy, zealous Y-types. We may land up in a perfect world when we die. In the meantime, we have to deal with the X-types. The traditional response to the X-types is to have tight control, close monitoring, minimal delegation and clear rewards and punishments for success and failure. There are still plenty of bosses who will assume that everyone who works for them is an X-type. They are highly controlling and demanding. They may not be fun to work for, but they can work their way up the career ladder.

Y-types can be managed differently. They can be trusted to do their best as committed colleagues. Trust, empowerment and delegation take the place of control.

This exploration of the X and Y worlds is based on McGregor's *The Human Side of Enterprise* (1960), which remains a classic description of different types of motivation at work. Increasingly, much of the world is moving from X to Y. The cynical, untrusting world of the X-type is perhaps typical of the nineteenth-century sweatshop where uneducated masses were hired for their hands, not their brains. The bosses bossed and the workers worked. In some cases the workers revolted and got exploited by tyrannical governments instead of tyrannical capitalists. In the West, the workers got educated. So now we see more of the theory Y world, where workers work in offices and with their brains. We need more than compliance – we need commitment. We need employees' talent to work through the increasing complexity and confusion of modern employment.

> What works for the worker should also work for the leader.

McGregor focused on the worker. But what works for the worker should also work for the leader. Although the world may be moving from X to Y, many managers feel much more comfortable in X mode. Look at the two types of management in the table and decide which you are. Also, decide which type of boss you would prefer to work for.

Types of management

Management criteria	X-type manager	Y-type leader
Basis of power	Formal authority	Authority and respect
Focus of control	Process compliance	Outcomes, achievement
Communication style	One-way: tell and do	Two-way: tell and listen
Success criteria	Make no mistakes	Beat targets
Attention to detail	High	Moderate

Management criteria	X-type manager	Y-type leader
Ambiguity tolerance	Minimal	Moderate
Political ability	Moderate	High
Preferred structure	Hierarchy	Network

Many people instinctively prefer the more inspirational Y-type leader. I have worked for both. The Y-type leader was much more demanding. They may forgive the occasional mistake, but overall their expectations are much higher. The X-type was a mean and nasty apology for a manager. But working for him was a simple matter of keeping your nose clean, doing what you were told and no more, and being blindly loyal and obedient. He expected compliance, not commitment. The Y-type expected commitment and would tolerate occasional non-compliance if that helped achieve a goal.

The catch is that both types of leader can succeed, in the right context. The X-type manager succeeds in a classic machine bureaucracy where the emphasis is on avoiding mistakes and achieving predictability and control. Systems integration houses, insurance companies and large parts of the public sector fit this style.

The Y-type leader fits where there is a need to change and to adapt to different and uncertain customer and competitive pressures. This better describes creative agencies, entrepreneurial organisations and professional service firms. The Y-type leader explodes in the X-type environment and vice versa. You have to find the environment where your style will work.

Practical theories of motivation: part two

McGregor's X- and Y-types find an echo in Herzberg's two-factor theory of motivation. As a leader, he argued, you can motivate people in one of two ways. Pick the option below that you think works in your organisation.

Option one

Make sure individuals have the status and title and terms and conditions they deserve. Pay for performance and pay a bonus for over-performance. Use hours, holidays, flexitime and family-friendly work policies to get the right balance of staff. This is classic rational management. It is the sort of thing that public sector unions like to discuss with public sector employers.

The problem with option one is that this is a never-ending treadmill. Once someone has got the pay rise and the bonus, then they want the shorter working hours. Herzberg called these 'hygiene factors'. In practice, not only do they do little to motivate but they can be demotivators too. Bad pay and conditions demotivate; good pay and conditions are never sufficient to produce stellar performance.

Despite this, many organisations still use pay and bonuses as a substitute for management or motivation. Pay discussions sound very managerial: senior executives sit round a table discussing people (like managers should) and performance (like managers should) and make decisions (like managers should) about money (very managerial). And at the end of several hours in a sweaty room and locked in mortal combat over the bonus scheme, they successfully irritate everyone. Pay a successful trader or fund manager a £100,000 bonus and they may promptly resign (after the money is in their bank account) when they find that one of their peers has received a £120,000 bonus. From the company's perspective, the bonus, in theory if not in practice, measures the worth of an individual's contribution. From the individual's perspective, it measures their worth against their peers. No one likes being told that they are worth less than someone else, especially if they have the city-sized ego of a trader or fund manager.

> No one likes being told that they are worth less than someone else.

Option two

Focus on the intrinsic rewards, recognition and value of the job, creating a sense of community and belonging. This can achieve exceptional results at exceptionally low cost. Many vocational careers, such as the army, teaching and academia, pay poorly but can attract exceptional talent and achieve exceptional results. Some of the best and brightest graduates go off to work as underpaid researchers for politicians or work for peanuts in the glamorous world of the international auction houses.

The choice between these two options goes to the heart of current discussions about stress, employee protection and regulation. The received wisdom is that employees need to be protected by regulation from the harsh winds of the marketplace. Flexitime, family-friendly policies and shorter working weeks are all part of this trend. There are few people who would want to reverse this. The public sector sets the best practice example in terms of working hours, flexitime and being family friendly. It also suffers by far the highest rates of absenteeism, sickness and stress-related complaints. Focusing on option one may be important, but in the case of the public sector, it is clearly not enough to motivate staff.

Conversely, it is clear that many people are quite happy to seek out what appear to be stressful careers. The modern professions, from accounting to law, consulting and finance, all put new graduates through sweat-it-out apprenticeships. And they are overwhelmed with demand for positions. These are classic option two-type careers: the hours may be antisocial and the demands may be extreme, but the opportunities are great. If people see that they are doing something worthwhile in an organisation that has prospects and they have some control over their future, that goes a long way to making up for the lack of an on-site crèche. Conversely, put someone in an organisation under siege (much of the public sector), with limited career prospects and limited autonomy, and the only sources of motivation are essentially option one-type bribes: more money, easier conditions. This is fertile ground for strikes and conflict.

For the leader, this contrast between option one and option two is critical. The easy way out for all leaders is to go down option one routes: more money, easy terms. The motivation lasts as long as it takes for the bonus to hit the bank account. The harder route, but the one that sustains motivation longer, is option two: give people meaningful work, create a sense of belonging, opportunity and recognition, and you are more likely to motivate. The cynics will argue that you will be able to exploit people better – more work for modest pay.

> Create a sense of belonging, opportunity and recognition.

As a leader in the middle of the organisation, there is not much you can do to change option one. You have to make the most of the hand you have been dealt by the organisation. You have to deploy some of the motivational skills in option two.

Teach First: making a motivational offering

At first sight, Teach First had perhaps the least attractive recruiting proposition ever devised for top graduates. It asked them to do two years' teaching in the most challenging schools in the country with some of the most disadvantaged children. They received six weeks' training, which meant giving up any chance of a holiday after graduation. They would be paid about half what they would receive if they joined a top-flight consulting firm. Teach First lacked the prestige of the big recruiters. It was a start-up – no one had heard of it. It was a charity. It had a tiny budget.

In its first year, more than 5% of Oxbridge and Imperial final-year undergraduates had applied. At the time, no graduates from these universities were teaching in the target schools. Since 2014 it has become the number one graduate recruiter in the UK. Dropout rates are low and the enthusiasm of the new teachers is high, despite the huge stress and challenges they face on a daily basis.

Why should high-flying graduates be motivated to join such an unlikely scheme, against better-paid offerings, and why did they feel motivated to stay in the scheme even after the reality of working in the challenging schools became clear?

The good news is that there are graduates out there who have strong social values. Teach First gave them a chance to make a worthwhile contribution. But that was never going to be enough. They may have hearts, but they also have heads. Teach First is designed to develop graduates into leaders of the future. It gives them far more practical experience of core leadership skills, such as motivating, influencing, dealing with conflict and surviving adversity, than any amount of staring at computer screens will do. Trading bonds or writing reports may make money, but at the end of two years it will be the Teach First participants who are prepared for leadership, not the highly paid galley slaves chained to their computers.

To make this promise credible, many top recruiters in consulting, investment banking and law support Teach First. The participants do not get huge pay and they do not get lengthy holidays. They do very poorly on Herzberg's option one route: good money and easy hours. They do very well on option two: they have a meaningful job, they have real prospects, they are highly recognised and they are given high autonomy and responsibility. Option two is very hard work for the employer and the employed. It can have dramatic results.

Practical theories of motivation: part three

Life is a little more subtle than flipping a coin and choosing between X and Y. Different people have different needs at different times.

I learned about how needs differ at an early stage. I set out for India in search of enlightenment. I got to Afghanistan and ran out of money. This was in the days before there were mobile phones for the emotionally incontinent and credit cards for the financially feckless.

My interest in enlightenment plummeted and my interest in money soared. So I sold my blood, but not my soul, to the locals. I got money, not enlightenment, and was grateful for it.

For the rich and successful, survival is taken for granted. Many seek immortality by buying up art collections, endowing charities and naming universities, buildings and departments after themselves. Most of us are in between those two extremes most of the time. We want to be paid, we want to feel a sense of belonging to something worthwhile and we would like to be recognised for what we do.

Perhaps all this is obvious. So it is refreshing to find that this is a case of practical theory from Maslow's hierarchy of needs (see Figure 13.1).

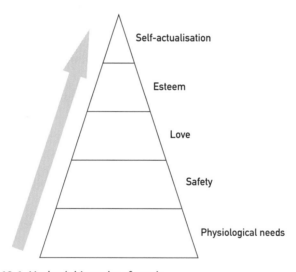

Figure 13.1 Maslow's hierarchy of needs
Source: Maslow, A.H. (1943) 'A theory of human motivation', *Psychological Review* 50(4), 370–96. This content is in the public domain.

Maslow argued that we are all needs junkies. We want to climb the ladder of needs from survival to immortality. Let us climb the ladder with him, converting his language into the language of leaders.

- **Physiological needs** for Maslow are items such as food and water: without them we become hungry and thirsty. Pay and conditions are the food and water of the employment world.

- **Safety** is a sense of security which comes in part from the employer and also from knowing that you have the skills to do the job. If the worst comes to the worst, they are skills you can use elsewhere.

- **Love** can be dangerous at work. So instead of loving your staff, it is enough to make sure that they have a sense of belonging and community, that they are trusted and respected for who they are. At its most basic, this is about leaders taking a positive interest in the careers and lives of those they are responsible for.

- **Esteem** is about recognising and rewarding individuals. The old saying holds true: 'Praise in public, criticise in private.' One leader makes sure that he praises ten times as often as he criticises. Sometimes he finds it difficult. But once you start looking, there is usually much to praise and be thankful for.

- **Self-actualisation** is about achievement – creating a legacy that is meaningful and recognised.

If you asked a leader what each rung of Maslow's hierarchy of needs was about, they would not know. But effective leaders understand this model intuitively, and they play to it.

An unauthorised version of the model converted into the reality of the workplace is shown in Figure 13.2.

Everyone has something more they want. Everyone has something they fear. We fear a project going wrong, or a supplier or staff member failing us. We fear losing our jobs sometimes. We fear being left behind by our peers in the leadership marathon. There is always something we fear.

> We fear being left behind by our peers in the leadership marathon.

Figure 13.2 Maslow's hierarchy of needs (the unauthorised, revisionist, leadership version)

> There is also always something we want.

There is also always something we want. Perhaps many of us would really like to become billionaires, Oscar winners, sports stars or astronauts. All at the same time. But these things are not easy. We are always making a trade-off between what we want and the risk and effort involved in getting there. We are risk averse (we fear failure) and we prefer things to be made easier, not more difficult.

Some leaders use the fear part of the equation most. Fear-based leaders stress the negative: 'If you don't …' or 'You can't afford to get this wrong.' In the short term, this can be highly effective. Eventually, however, people burn out, stress out and walk out. Meanwhile, the fear-based leader has achieved results and may well have moved onwards and upwards to greater things. They climb to the top over the career corpses of those they have killed.

Other leaders use the greed element most. Greed is not just about money, it is about ego, recognition and immortality. Having a professorial chair or a museum named after you is greed fulfilled, for a while. Even at the top of a career, there is hunger for something more: most CEOs are not content to be mere custodians of a legacy they have inherited. They want to create their own legacy. They crave more recognition. This way, disaster can lie. The lure of greatness is a distraction from the obligation to deliver.

Finally, good leaders use idleness to their advantage in two ways. First, good leaders do not make life difficult for their followers. They are clear about what they want, where they are going and how to get there. They give structure and guidance to their teams to minimise wasted effort. They help clear the way forward with the rest of the organisation by removing political obstacles and aligning other parts of the organisation with what they are trying to achieve. They set their followers up for success. Second, good leaders do not interfere with their teams. They do not over-manage. They give teams discretion within a structure. The leader risks looking idle, because they let go. This is a hard lesson for many leaders to learn.

One popular form of good leadership is 'MBWA', or Management By Walking Around. MBWA can create the 'leader in the locker room' problem. Arguably, the opposite of MBWA is required: Management By Walking Away. For a leader, this is nerve-racking – you direct a team to do something and you want to see how it is doing. You want to pull up the seed every few moments to see how it is progressing. Leave it alone. Be available for help, but do not interfere. The end result may not be exactly what you predicted; it may be better. By not interfering, you show you trust the team, they feel motivated, they do their best and they learn more by trying to do things themselves than by blindly following your exact orders.

Maslow can be complicated. In practice, leaders cannot go round calculating whether each person is at the love stage or the self-actualisation stage, let alone know what to do about it. Going into a boardroom and asking which board members are at the love level would be original, if not totally advisable or actionable. The simpler way is to remember three things: fear, greed and idleness.

> **Work on people's hopes. Work on people's fears.**

Work on people's hopes. Work on people's fears – humane leaders seek to remove risk and remove fear; inhumane leaders happily stoke up fear. Finally, put idleness to work. Make things easy for others: give a clear structure and direction. Make it easy for yourself: do not over-manage. Fear, greed and idleness work as much for selling ideas as they do for motivating people. If your idea appeals to someone's hopes and removes a fear, and you make it easy for them to say 'yes', they are likely to say 'yes'.

Leaders may not understand or care for the theory. They just put it into practice.

How to motivate your team

1 **Show you care for each member of the team, and for their career**
   Invest time to understand their hopes, fears and dreams. Casual time by the coffee machine, not a formal meeting in an office, is the best way to get to know your team members.

2 **Say thank you**
   We all crave recognition: we want to know that we are doing something worthwhile and we are doing it well. Make your praise real, for real achievement. And make it specific. Avoid the synthetic one-minute manager praise ('Gee, you typed that email really well').

3 **Never demean a team member**
   If you have any criticism, keep it private and make it constructive. Don't scold your team members like schoolchildren: treat them as partners and work together to find a way forward.

4   Delegate well

Delegate meaningful work that will stretch and develop your team member. Yes, there is routine rubbish to be delegated, but delegate some of the interesting stuff as well. Be clear and consistent about your expectations.

5   Have a clear vision

Show where your team is going and how each team member can help you all get there. Have a clear vision for each team member: know where they are going and how they can develop their careers.

6   Trust your team

Do not micro manage them. Have the courage to implement MBWA: Management By Walking Away.

7   Be honest

That means having difficult, but constructive, conversations with struggling team members. Don't hide or shade the truth. Honesty builds trust and respect.

8   Set clear expectations

Be very clear about promotion prospects, bonuses and the required outcome of each piece of work. Assume you will be misunderstood: people hear what they want to hear. So make it simple and repeat it often and be consistent.

9   Over-communicate

You have two ears and one mouth: use them in that proportion. Listen twice as much as you speak. Then you will find out what is really going on and what drives your team members, and you can act accordingly.

10 Don't try to be friends

It is more important to be respected than liked: trust endures while popularity is fickle and leads to weak compromises. If your team members trust and respect you, they will want to work for you.

Chapter 14

Motivate your team: practice

We have looked at what the theory of leadership says. Now let's hear what leaders say about human nature.

First, in our survey of more than 1,000 current and emerging leaders, we found the most important quality valued in a leader was the ability to motivate others. When we asked our participants how satisfied they were with the motivational capabilities of their leaders, we found a huge motivation gap. Although motivation was seen as the most important attribute of a leader, only 37% were satisfied with the performance of their leaders in this respect. Clearly, there is a problem for many leaders, but an opportunity for you. If you can motivate your team, you will be ahead of your peers and respected by your team.

> If you can motivate your team, you will be ahead of your peers and respected by your team.

We looked further to find out more about what people expected in terms of motivation, and then we looked at specific situations to see how well or poorly they were handled.

We asked people about leaders who had motivated them and leaders who had not motivated them. This is what they expected from a boss:

- My boss shows an interest in me and my career.
- I trust my boss: (s)he is honest with me.
- I know where we are going and how to get there.
- I am doing a worthwhile job.
- I am recognised for my contribution.

We will look at each briefly. But first let's look at what is not there:

- **Money.** When it was mentioned, it was seen as a demotivator, not a motivator. Get the money wrong and you send a signal either that you cannot be trusted to deliver on a promise or that you do not value the person highly enough relative to their peers. Either way, you have broken trust and your credibility as a leader of that person is lost.
- **Family-friendly hours, shorter hours, flexitime, facilities.** These simply did not appear on the radar screen. People who have signed up for the leadership journey have signed up for some self-sacrifice and are also good at compartmentalising their lives. They do not share personal concerns in a professional environment. If they have doubts, they conceal them until they have decided to leave.

Look again at the list of expectations that followers have of leaders when it comes to motivation. It is very simple. There are no dark arts to be learned in leading people. Treat them and care for them as humans and the chances are that they will respond. We will look at each expectation in turn.

My boss shows an interest in me and my career

Hierarchical relationships are unequal. You are more important to your followers than they are to you. Their jobs and livelihoods depend on you: the reverse is only partially and indirectly true. It also means that you probably focus intently on managing your boss, but less intently on managing downwards. Most people know more about their bosses than they do about their followers.

As a follower, if your boss is clearly not interested in your career, it is unnerving.

Normally, there is an implicit psychological contract between leader and follower, which is far more important than any job description. The contract says that the follower will do what it takes to support the leader, and the leader will look after the pay, promotion and assignment prospects of the follower. If the leader is either unwilling or unable to deliver on the leader's half of the contract, there is little incentive for the follower to feel good about following.

Some leaders make this contract highly explicit. In return they demand absolute loyalty. They create a personal fiefdom. At promotion and bonus councils they will play very hard to deliver the promises they made to their teams. The result can be dysfunctional: a power baron with their own team emerges, playing to their own rules, with their own team. The team will tend to show great loyalty to a leader who looks after them so well. The team becomes a cult: inward looking, demanding and divisive with the rest of the organisation.

As a boss, the simplest way to show an interest in each of your team members is to use a vital and now familiar tool: listen to them. Understand their hopes and fears, what they can and cannot do, how they like to work and what they want to achieve. You can then have conversations about assignments, performance and expectations which respect them and their needs. This lets you achieve a vital transition: you can move from managing your agenda to managing your team. As leaders, it is easy to think that managing your agenda is a substitute for managing your team. In fact, the two things are quite different.

Showing an interest in your team members is not about pleasing them or being weak. If you have a real interest in them, you will have early and difficult conversations about expectations (workload, bonus and promotion prospects) and performance. The earlier the conversation happens, the easier it is to be constructive about it and find workable solutions. These conversations may not help you in terms of popularity, but they will help you hugely in terms of trust and respect. Trust and respect are sounder currencies than popularity.

> Trust and respect are sounder currencies than popularity.

By taking time to listen to and understand each of your team members, you will be well ahead of many of your peers. You will be seen as a good boss to work for.

I trust my boss: (s)he is honest with me

'Honesty' and 'business' are words that are not often heard together in the media. But all the leaders I interviewed, even in industries such as investment banking, stressed honesty. This is not about honour and ethics and being nice to the planet, this is much more hard-faced and practical.

Followers want to know where they stand. If they have been working hard for a year and think they are doing fine, it is devastating if the boss turns up at the annual review and gives an unsatisfactory ranking. The boss has been dishonest. Dishonesty is not about lying, it is about failing to tell the whole truth, even the uncomfortable truth, promptly. This is an honesty test that would cause panic for some politicians.

Honesty is ultimately about trust – if you do not trust someone, it becomes very hard to work for them as a leader.

I know where we are going and how to get there

Sometimes this is called 'vision'. But vision is too grand: it sounds like Moses, Martin Luther King and Gandhi all rolled together. It is easier than that. A vision is your idea of the

IPA agenda, framed as a story. Provide a simple description of where your team has to get to on the next three-month project. Let your people know what they need to develop personally over the next six months and the practical actions they can take to develop those skills. Show where your business is going over the next one to three years. Do these things and you start to give people the clarity, structure and direction they need. Put it the other way: if your people do not know where they are going or how they are going to get there, they are soon going to become very frustrated.

> Give people the clarity, structure and direction they need.

I am doing a worthwhile job

Not everyone gets to do exciting, high-powered jobs all the time. Some jobs are plain dull, tedious, stressful or unglamorous. But they need to be done.

The world of repairing shoes is perhaps not the most exciting. Go to a shoe repair shop and the conditions are hardly brilliant. Some of them are little more than holes in the wall. Staff tend to be on wages that are modest by any standards and would be small change for a banker. Yet John Timpson manages to create a loyal workforce in his shoe repair shops and he is widely regarded as a very good leader. One of the many things he does is to focus on customer satisfaction and constantly recognise and reward great service – he always has a supply of prizes available in his car. He makes sure that he praises at least ten times more than he criticises. His staff focus on the positive impact they are having on customers – each happy customer is evidence that they are doing a worthwhile job.

In investment banking there are plenty of dull jobs to be done in checking documents, but the dullness is offset by knowing that a billion-pound deal may fail if you get it wrong. Even dull stuff can be made worthwhile in the right context.

I am recognised for my contribution

Let's make this simple. If you never get any recognition for all your efforts, you get upset. You probably do not feel terribly motivated to put in more effort. So recognise the efforts of your team. Some leaders feel the need to grab all the glory if their teams do well; they are also the leaders who are the first to walk away and delegate blame if things go wrong. Strong leaders have the self-confidence to recognise the success of their teams.

Recognising success is effective because:

● it shows the leader has built a strong and effective team

● it motivates the team.

Recognition takes multiple forms: it can be as simple as a few well-chosen words in front of the CEO. Take time to say thank you, and to mean it, to the individual or team directly. Recognition can also be prizes, newsletter mentions or celebrations during a night out. Pay rises are often the least effective form of recognition because in most organisations they are not public knowledge.

Chapter 15

Motivation and moments of truth

In any relationship there are moments of truth. This is when you discover the real nature of the other person. The moment of truth can come at any time. It is the moment both sides discover whether they can trust each other. Typically, these moments of trust come in two forms:

1 Payback time: can you deliver on the psychological contract?

2 Problem time: how will you deal with the screaming monkeys?

Payback time

As a leader you are making an implicit, sometimes explicit, promise to look after the interests of your followers. Fail to deliver for them and you are a failure, not a leader, to them.

We have already seen how some leaders play hardball for their followers at promotion and bonus time. One budding power baron played this game to perfection. Essentially, he rigged the process. He worked out all the evaluation criteria and wrote evaluations that were designed to score maximum points for his followers. Anyone who had been disloyal got a lousy evaluation, even if they were very good. He then backed his evaluations all the way. It was impossible to argue with him – his followers had only worked for him so there was no other point of view. The only benchmarks were the lousy reviews he had written for disloyal people who had gone on to succeed elsewhere: this was evidence, he claimed, that his evaluation criteria were tougher than anyone else's. He delivered results to his teams, who wisely remained loyal to him.

Other promises are just as important.

Developing trust

Once, I found myself earning real sweat equity in Riyadh, Saudi Arabia. The project went well. The client wanted to go to a second stage. The partner came in at the end of the first project expecting to agree the second stage with the client. I dreaded the meeting: I had planned a great holiday as an escape from all the hard work. The partner knew this, but I could see economic necessity would outweigh personal need. The moment of truth came. The client agreed to the second stage and my heart sank.

Then the partner turned to the client and said, 'Of course, you don't mind starting phase two later so that Jo can have his holiday, do you?'

The client was delighted: suddenly he saw me as a human (you can fool some of the people ...), not just a work drudge. My relationship with the client improved. More importantly, I realised I had discovered a partner I could trust. We worked together on and off for the next ten years.

Always deliver on expectations. This means you must be careful what you say because your team will hear what they want to hear. When you say, 'I hope/intend/will try to get you your promotion/bonus/improved budget', your team will hear you say, 'I will ...' Your vague promise of help will be taken as a firm commitment to deliver. If you don't deliver, your excuses will fall on deaf ears. Delivering on expectations means you must manage expectations well.

> Always deliver on expectations. This means you must be careful what you say.

Problem time: the screaming monkeys

This test is a very easy one to fail. It happens when staff come to you with a problem. Like any good leader, you make sure that you are available for advice. So you are pleased to see someone come through your open door with a problem. You are even more pleased when they walk back out of the door with the problem lifted from their shoulders. Congratulations. You have just failed the test. Failed? When I did everything right? Are you nuts?

Let's call up the slow-motion replay and see why the referee awarded the penalty against you.

A member of staff comes into your office. She has a monkey on her back. It is a screaming monkey and behaving badly. She needs help. So you take the monkey off her back. You now have the monkey and she leaves happy. Hearing that you are in a good mood, another staffer comes in. He has two screaming monkeys, one on each shoulder. You lift the burden from his shoulders. You now have three screaming monkeys in your office. By the end of the day, you have a vast troupe of monkeys in your office. Your staff are very happy, and you are very unhappy.

The leader is not there to solve every problem. You have assembled a team to solve the problems for you. You may have the most expertise, but avoid the temptation to become the leader in the locker room. You need to raise your game and focus on the wider issues facing the team – making sure they are working on the right problem, making sure you have the right team, making sure they have the right support and development. Only if you force them to solve the problem themselves will they develop the skills and confidence to become effective.

> Only if you force them to solve the problem themselves will they develop the skills and confidence to become effective.

When the staff member comes into the office with a monkey, give them advice and coaching on how to deal with the monkey. This is neither quick nor easy. It will take careful questioning to understand their problem and to help them understand it properly as well. It is probably easier in the short term to deal with the problem yourself, to take the monkey off their backs. But make sure they deal with the monkey themselves. If you are really smart, invite them to take away one of your own monkeys as well. It could be a good development opportunity for them. By the end of the day, you will have succeeded if there are no more screaming monkeys in your room.

The essence of this approach is to help people through their problems, not to solve their problems even if you think you know the answer. If you solve all their problems for them, they will never learn or develop as individuals. Neither will they have any ownership over your solution; they will lack commitment and belief. Coaching them through their problem helps them learn and develop and it ensures that they have ownership of whatever solution they eventually discover. As they become more adept at solving problems themselves, so they will rely less on coming to you for help. In the short term, coaching is high effort, but it pays big long-term dividends.

Chapter 16

Delegate well

How many real working hours can you reliably deliver every day? Some people like to claim that they sleep for just a few hours each night and always work 16 hours a day, 7 days a week. Even if they are telling the truth (which they are not), their claims show that they are poor leaders. Any good leader can deliver far more than 24 working hours in a day. If you build the right team, they can collectively deliver thousands of hours of work every day. Your job is not to do all the work yourself, it is to make sure that your team can accomplish what needs to be done. That means you need the right team, and you need to delegate to the team.

Of course, there are plenty of reasons you should not delegate. Here are some of the reasons that I typically hear:

● I can do it better myself.

● It is faster for me to do it.

● This is too important.

● Only I have the skills for this.

These excuses need a translation. Here is what the team hears when these excuses are trotted out:

● I can do it better myself: I don't trust my team to do it well.

● It is faster for me to do it: I don't trust my team to do it fast.

● This is too important: I don't trust my team to do it at all.

● Only I have the skills for this: I think my team is incompetent.

Poor delegation is a sign of a poor leader who does not trust the team they have. And who is at fault if the team is weak? Occasionally, leaders need to look in the mirror. If you lack trust in your team, you have the wrong team.

If you don't delegate to your team, your team will know they are not trusted and their morale will plummet. The less you delegate, the less they learn and grow. That creates a vicious circle where you cannot delegate because they do not have the skills, and they do not have the skills because you do not delegate.

> If you don't delegate to your team, your team will know they are not trusted and their morale will plummet.

Here is why it makes sense to delegate:

- You can focus on where you add most value.
- Your team will learn and grow and become a better team.
- You run the risk they may come up with a better solution than the one you thought of.
- You create more hours in the day and can sleep at night.
- You will motivate your team by showing you trust them: trust is a two-way street.

The art of delegation has two parts: what you should delegate and how you should delegate.

What you should delegate

If you ask 'What can I delegate?', you may come up with a short list. Instead, ask 'What can I not delegate under any circumstances?' This will do two things for you. First, it will define where you add most value and what your true role is. It will help you focus on what matters most. Second, it will enable you to delegate everything else. As we have seen earlier, the list of things that a leader cannot delegate is fairly short. You cannot delegate appraisals, negotiating budgets, hiring and firing the right team; you should also expect to run political interference and to protect and promote your team as necessary.

Don't delegate the blame when things go wrong.

There is just one other thing you should not delegate: don't delegate the blame when things go wrong, unless you want to create a finger-pointing, political and back-stabbing culture in your team. Don't play the blame game. It is better to learn than to judge. Learn what went wrong and why, then move on. The blame game is about changing perceptions of the past. Learning is about preparing for a better future.

It is standard practice to feel nervous about delegating important tasks to people who may not have the same level of experience as you do. But reflect on how you have grown and developed. You have succeeded because you have taken on challenges that stretched you. Given a challenge, most teams will relish the chance to shine. They will rise to the occasion if you support them well.

Be brave: if in doubt, delegate.

Delegation heaven and hell

Heaven

Paul was one of the most idle leaders I had ever met. He was also very successful and everyone wanted to work with him. This was highly irritating to all his colleagues who worked harder and were less successful and less in demand as a boss. His secret was that he delegated more or less everything. He knew precisely where he could add value: he was great at selling to clients, and he was great at making sure he got the right resources and budget. Once he had secured his clients, team and budget he let the team get on with it, with minimal interference. His teams responded well to this vote of confidence in their ability by working hard to deliver great results. They learned and grew in the process. The clients got a great outcome and Paul got his bonus. Everyone was happy.

Hell

David thought he was a great manager and leader. He thought so highly of himself that he realised everyone else simply was not up to his standards. No matter who came onto his teams, they all failed to live up to David's expectations, even people who were exceptionally successful both before and after working on one of his teams.

Because he did not trust his teams, he delegated as little as possible. He even controlled access to the photocopy machine. When he did delegate, it would be a mixture of routine rubbish (standard reports to be completed) and an occasional hospital pass, a project that was already so badly astray that it would fail and land you in career hospital. In this way, he was very good at delegating the blame.

When he did delegate, he liked to keep tight control. He knew that good managers should always be in control. This meant frequent reports, combined with frequent changes of direction. One of his professional frustrations was that he found it increasingly hard to get good people to work on his teams, which he put down to the incompetence of the HR group.

How you should delegate

Delegating requires answering the same journalist questions you have to ask when you are building a plan: what, when, why, who and how. Here is what each question means:

- **What?** What is the goal? How will we know when we have succeeded?

- **When?** What are the key milestones and checkpoints that will let us know we are on track? When and how often do you require an update to check on progress?

- **Why?** Why is this important and to who? Give your team some context so they can understand the challenge and its priorities.

- **Who?** Who are the team members and what are their roles?
- **How?** How will we go about doing this? What are the obstacles? Let your team raise concerns and explore how to overcome them. Delegation should be a dialogue, not a command.

This is not rocket science. But it is very easy for managers to just tell someone to do something and then move on. Remember though, your team are not psychic: they will not know the full context that you know, they will not know your expectations about how the task will be completed and they may not fully understand exactly what you want. Be ready to invest time to make sure they really understand what you want – avoiding misunderstanding avoids errors and wasted time later on.

> Be ready to invest time to make sure your team really understand what you want.

Check that your team understands what you want. That means more than asking 'Do you understand?' A mumbled 'yes' normally means 'not really'. There are two good signs of understanding. The first is when they paraphrase back to you what you have asked for. If they have misunderstood, their paraphrase will make that clear. The second positive sign is when they start challenging you about what, how and why the task should be done. This shows that they are listening and understanding, even if they are not yet agreeing with what you say. This active response is preferable to a passive response in which they say and do nothing. This normally means that they disagree with you or do not understand you, but either way they are not prepared to tell you.

Chapter 17

Coach your team for performance

C oaching is different from informal feedback. Informal feedback is a classic boss-to-team-member interaction: a judgement is being made and support is offered. Coaching is a longer-term journey aimed at longer-term improvement.

Coaching is not just for coaches. Every good leader needs to bring out the best in their team, and that requires a mixture of formal and informal feedback, mentoring and coaching. The essence of coaching is to enable someone to work through a challenge, find a solution and act on it – coaching is not about giving solutions or feedback. When someone discovers their own solution, they are more committed to it, more likely to act on it and more likely to learn from it. For a leader who wants to avoid the monkey problem (above), coaching is a vital performance skill.

> The essence of coaching is to enable someone to work through a challenge, find a solution and act on it.

Coaching can be thought of as an event and a journey. A coaching event is where a team member comes and asks for help. The coaching journey is about helping that same individual grow and progress over a year or more. A coaching event is part of the coaching journey.

A coaching event can be reduced to the five Os:

1 Objectives.

2 Overview.

3 Options.

4 Obstacles.

5 Outcomes.

These five Os give a simple and natural structure to an effective coaching conversation. Let's look at each in turn:

- **Objectives**. Be clear about what you want to achieve. If you want someone to do something in a certain way, do not try to coach them into reading your mind: tell them. It pays to be clear about what the problem is that you are trying to solve. When you are presented with some symptoms of a problem, dig to find out the root causes of the problem rather than dealing with the symptoms alone. Dealing with symptoms not causes is as pointless as using spot remover to help a child with measles.

- **Overview**. Let your coachee lay out the situation as they see it. Even if it is a flawed perspective, they will want their voice to be heard and respected. Then encourage them to look at the same situation from the perspective of other players. If they are complaining about the behaviour of another department or individual, get them to explore what the situation looks like from the other person's perspective. As you consider different perspectives, you will understand the problem better and you may well be encouraging them to feel their way towards some solutions.

- **Options**. Encourage the coachee to explore a range of options: you want to avoid the 'my way or no way' syndrome which often leads to conflict, not progress. Avoid discussions about who is right or wrong – that is to look to the past, not the future. Help them look to the future. Even if the future looks bleak, there are normally one or two things that anyone can do to make some progress and achieve some stability in an unstable position. Exploring options is about the art of the possible, not about what cannot be done. As the coachee explores different options, you will normally find that one emerges as the most sensible way forward. You may already have thought of the solution, but let the coachee discover it so that they own it.

- **Obstacles.** This is the reality check. Before agreeing to the course of action, ask a simple question: 'What might stop this happening?' You want to avoid having someone run off with great enthusiasm which is dashed by the first obstacle they encounter. Help them identify, prepare for and deal with these challenges in advance.

- **Outcomes**. Ask the coachee to summarise the outcomes of the session. They should summarise both what they have learned and what action they are going to take. The purpose of the summary is to check for understanding and to help fix the key points in the mind of both coachee and coach.

None of this is rocket science. You do not need to go on a five-day course and be certified by some self-important institution in order to have a coaching conversation. You simply need to know how to have a sensible, structured conversation with the person you are coaching. The five Os model gives a simple framework for your coaching conversation. As you have the conversation, remember one more O: open questions. As a coach, your goal is not to give the answer but to help the other person hit upon the answer. They may even hit upon a better answer than the one you were thinking of in the first place.

> Know how to have a sensible, structured conversation with the person you are coaching.

We have seen the importance of open versus closed questions in persuading (Chapter 7). They are also important in the context of coaching. An open coaching question is one to which there is no 'yes/no' answer: it forces the other person to give a fuller and more thoughtful response. A closed question invites a 'yes/no' answer and can quickly kill the conversation.

Open questions	Closed questions
What was their reaction?	Did they disagree?
What were they expecting?	Is that what they expected?
How did the sales meeting go?	Has the client agreed to our proposal yet?
How's the project going?	Have you finished the project yet?

The final secret of a good coach we have already come across a few times, and it is the secret coaches share with great leaders and great sales people: they all have two ears and one mouth, and they all use them in that proportion. The more you listen, the better you are likely to be doing.

Coaching from failure to success

Chris was a promising young batsman for his county. There was talk of him becoming an England player one day. To improve his chances, he decided to get some help from the senior batsmen in his county. They were all more than happy to help. Each one advised him on how to hold the bat, how to stand, how to move, how to deal with different types of ball, how to read what the bowler was about to do.

The more advice he got, the worse his performance became. Far from getting into the England side, he was struggling to hold his place in the county team. His career was heading towards extinction.

Ed, one of the county bowlers, noticed what was happening. Ed was pretty much useless as a batsman, but decided to help Chris anyway. Chris's heart sank: things could only get worse from here.

The first thing Ed did was to tell Chris to ignore all the advice from the senior batsmen. 'They are not telling you how to bat well, they are telling you how they bat. They all bat in different ways, so they are all going to be giving you conflicting advice. No wonder you look like a confused circus contortionist when you come out to bat.'

The lights went on in Chris's mind. The senior batsmen had not been coaching him at all: they had assumed that how they batted was the only way to bat. They did not realise that different batsmen could succeed in different ways. Over the coming weeks, Ed helped Chris rediscover his natural strengths and build on those. Because Ed was a useless batsman, he did not try to give any technical advice, he let Chris discover what worked for him. Over the rest of the season, Chris got steadily better and once again the dreams of an England place became more realistic.

As leaders, we need to recognise that our formula for successful leadership is not universal. There are many ways to succeed. Let your team members discover what works for them, rather than imposing your methods on them.

The coaching journey

Most coaching models fail because they go no further than creating a structure for an individual coaching session. This may help you coach someone through a specific challenge, but it is not enough. If, as a leader, you spend your time simply helping people resolve problems, you run into several issues:

- Your coaching becomes a random walk through random problems.
- Your coachee makes no systemic improvement to the way they think, perform or behave.
- Your coachee learns to be dependent on you, rather than learning to deal with challenges themselves.
- You work reactively to situations, rather than having a proactive agenda.

A successful coaching relationship is based on a structured journey with a beginning, middle and end. Before starting to coach any of your team, you need to agree with them what they want and need to achieve from the coaching relationship. You can agree this only if you both know where they start (what their needs and opportunities are) and where they are going (how they want to improve over the next year).

Once you have set clear objectives, you have purpose and direction to your coaching. You may also decide someone else might be a better coach for the goals you have agreed – if the goal is to help someone understand and manage organisation politics better and you are not a great politician yourself, find someone else to be the coach.

Once you have agreed goals for the coaching journey, the goals for each coaching session become simpler. Typically, you will have three goals for each coaching session:

1 **Address immediate challenges for the coachee**. Even though you have an overall goal set for the year, you should let the coachee raise issues of immediate concern even if they are not directly relevant to the longer-term goal. Long-term goals may be important, but the short-term challenges are urgent. Deal with them both.

2 **Review progress against the overall goal for the year**. Encourage the coachee to reflect on situations where they have needed the skills that you are trying to help them build. Let them learn from what they are doing successfully or less successfully in such situations.

3 **Review what went well, and what went less well, since you last met them**. In each case, find out why it went well or otherwise. The purpose of this third discussion is to help the coachee coach themselves. Most flawed coaching models are deficit models: they focus on what is broken. As a leader, you want your team to discover what they are doing well, what they are good at and how they can focus on their strengths. You also want them to build enough self-awareness of what they are doing and how they are doing it so that they can coach themselves.

Most coaching models focus only on the first of the three discussions above. The second and third elements differentiate a leader's coaching model from that of the professional coach. It gives you a much more positive and proactive approach to helping and building the strengths of your team than traditional coaching models.

At this point, the ever-growing ranks of professional coaches will howl in anger and protest. They will insist that only an impartial and independent person can be an effective coach. This is self-serving nonsense. A good leader has to be a good coach. Good coaching will help each team member achieve their best performance. It will also build the trust and confidence each team member has in you. By demonstrating that you care enough to help them, you build ties of loyalty and commitment that can be worth their weight in gold.

> Good coaching will help each team member achieve their best performance.

Chapter 18

Manage performance

Most corporate performance management systems do not manage performance, they track performance. Tracking performance is important and necessary, but it does not help you develop a high-performing team. You should defer to your corporate tracking systems and fill in all the MBO, KPI and annual assessment forms as required. If nothing else, when it comes to pay, bonus and promotion time, these are the essential documents that will make your case for you.

Once you have complied with the administrivia of your performance tracking systems, you are left with the challenge of performance managing your team. Many weaker leaders think that performance tracking is the same as performance management. As we shall see, they are very different.

Manage performance in three phases: before, during and after the event. The event might be a meeting, a project, or a 12-month period.

Before the event: the psychological contract

Before the event, follow the rules of delegation. Be clear about the what, who, when, how and why. You are not giving dictation at this point. It should be a two-way conversation about expectations. You want certain outcomes in a set time for a set budget. You need to hear whether this is seen to be possible, what support you may need to provide and what is expected in return. This forms the basis of a psychological contract between you and the team or team member. It may be informal, but it is at least as important as the formal requirements of the performance tracking systems. Formal systems are there to be gamed, and an informal contract is about trust. If you game the informal contract, you break trust. This is why you need to take time to make sure that the psychological contract is both fair and agreed – if you simply dictate it, it will be seen as another set of requirements which can be gamed if necessary.

> Make sure that the psychological contract is both fair and agreed.

During the event: less is more

As a child, I was given a tulip bulb as a present. This was very exciting. I decided to performance manage the bulb closely. At least once a day I would dig the bulb out of its earth and check on its progress. I would then cover it up again and put some more organic fertiliser (manure) on it. Needless to say, it never grew. This is how some leaders performance manage: they are always checking on their team and then dumping some management manure on them. Then they wonder why the team fails.

There are two problems with close control. First, the more you control, the less trust you show in your team. If you trust people, they will normally respond positively. I took a school leadership team to see Range Rovers being built. They were astonished that line workers appeared to have no supervision. They were supervising themselves – each work station on the line had huge amounts of performance data which they proudly displayed and explained to us. If things went wrong, each team member could stop the whole line. This is standard practice in any modern auto plant. It gives a level of autonomy to teams which many traditional leaders still fear and avoid.

The second problem is that the more you interfere, the more you create extra work. Each time you ask for an update, the team is going to spend time preparing the update and reacting to any words of wisdom you may have imparted to them. Each time you ask a question, that may generate more work; each time you make a suggestion, that also generates more work. More control means less trust, lower morale and more work for the team.

> The more you interfere, the more you create extra work.

You can minimise the amount of control by agreeing in advance the key dates or major milestones. That is when you should have your updates. And simply by walking around, you will know whether your team members are starting to look anxious, over-worked and stressed out. You will hear the danger signals both from your team and from others connected to it. If danger is looming, that is when you should step in with a view to supporting rather than just controlling.

Trust your team – you will work less and they will achieve more. It is the idler's way to successful performance management.

After the event: focus on learning and growth

We react differently to failure and success: neither set of reactions is useful in performance management terms. Failure is often met with denial, or a post mortem in which the game is to find a victim to blame. We have still not fully got past the mindset of the Medieval era when natural misfortunes would be blamed on a hapless old widow – she would be the witch to be burned or ducked or drowned. We still find it useful to have a scapegoat, although widows are no longer the default choice. These post mortems are profoundly unhelpful – little is learned, and the blame game fosters a culture of politicking and divisiveness.

Reactions to success are also unhelpful. We tend to regard success as normal – we are all brilliant, so naturally success will follow. Success is not natural. There are always obstacles to success: crises, chaos and cock-ups are more natural than a smoothly working machine that never goes wrong. Because we regard success as normal, we rarely take the time to learn from it.

Regardless of whether we succeed or fail, we should always ask why that happened. The goal is not to apportion blame or praise but to learn and to grow. A simple way of debriefing is to ask two questions: WWW and EBI.

WWW stands for What Went Well. To make it more powerful make it WWWW: What Went Well and Why it went well. You can do this in a team or alone. The trick is to catch yourself succeeding. Learn why you succeed, and you can do more of the same. If you have had a setback, you should still ask WWW. Even in setbacks,

> The trick is to catch yourself succeeding.

there will have been some things you did right. Focus on these positive actions and learn from them.

Only after you have answered WWW completely should you proceed to EBI: Even Better If .... Again, ask this in success or setbacks. There are always things you could have done better: figure out what you can do better and try that next time.

At no point do you need to challenge the team with the dreaded version of WWW: What Went Wrong. That is a negative and unhelpful question, which leads to unhelpful answers. EBI implicitly deals with what went wrong, but in a positive way by focusing on what can be done differently and better next time round.

Use this debrief to help the team learn and grow. When it becomes a habit, the capability of your team will grow fast and you will be doing real performance management.

From performance tracking to performance management

So far, we have taken the corporate performance tracking systems for granted. But no leader takes things for granted. You should question the annual appraisal process. In the words of quality guru W Edwards Deming, 'It (the appraisal system) nourishes short-term performance, annihilates long-term planning, builds fear, demolishes teamwork, nourishes rivalry and politics.' There is a better way forward: move from performance tracking to performance development. This is a fairly simple but powerful transformation. Instead of focusing on achievement (which is performance tracking), focus on development (which supports performance management). This sounds odd in theory, but is simple in practice. The table shows what the two approaches look like, taking the example of an assessment of a first-time manager who was promoted just 12 months ago.

Performance tracking for a new manager

	Below average	Average	Above average	Outstanding
Teamwork	✓			
Problem solving		✓		
People management	✓			
Strategic thinking		✓		
Delegation (etc.)	✓			

This assessment would be likely to cause meltdown. Telling a newly promoted manager that they are below average on most metrics would lead to a heated and adversarial discussion. There is always pressure to score people as above average. Typically, more than 80% of staff are assessed as above average. This is statistically impossible but emotionally inevitable. It also leads to overblown expectations. Performance tracking rarely leads to an honest conversation.

Now look at how the same evaluation might look using a development perspective.

Performance development for a new manager

	New manager	Developing manager	Maturing manager	Expert manager
Teamwork	✓			
Problem solving		✓		
People management	✓			
Strategic thinking		✓		
Delegation (etc.)	✓			

The ticks are all in the same boxes, but the result is completely different. Instead of having an argument, you are likely to have a constructive conversation. The new manager will not be surprised to see she is rated as a new manager in most categories, and may be pleasantly surprised to see she is already maturing in other categories. The conversation that follows is about how to continue to grow and develop over the next year. With this framework, you can ask each staff member to self-assess. This encourages reflection and normally leads to a reasonably accurate view of how each person is doing.

> The goal is to manage performance, not just track it.

The more radical option is to abolish the whole formal performance management system, which Adobe did in 2012. Adobe's goal is to stop managers hiding behind technology and forms, and to encourage them to have more frequent and honest check-ins with each staff member. In other words, the goal is to manage performance, not just track it. And that is what all good leaders should do.

Chapter 19

Leading professionals

Increasingly, leadership is about leading fellow professionals. This can be tough. Professionals can be high performance, but they are also high maintenance. Professionals often have high self-regard and do not care for being managed or led by anyone else. In the health service, doctors look down on managers; in professional service firms, the leaders are often the star revenue generators, not the star managers. So how do you lead people who do not want to be led and probably do not respect you beyond your ability to generate revenue?

> So how do you lead people who do not want to be led?

Here are ten ways in which you can make the most of your professionals:

1 **Stretch them**. Professionals are natural over-achievers. Let them over-achieve, learn and grow. An idle professional is a dangerous professional.

2 **Set a direction**. Professionals do not respect weak managers. Set a direction, be clear about how you will get there and stick to it.

3 **Shield your team**. Focus your team on where they can make a difference. Shield them from the politics, routine rubbish and noise of corporate life. They may even be grateful to you if you do this well.

4 **Support your team**. Set up the team for success: make sure they have the right resources, right support and right goal.

5 **Show you care**. Invest time in each team member: understand their needs and expectations. Help them on their career journey.

6 **No surprises**. Don't surprise your team at appraisal time: all trust will be lost. Have difficult performance conversations early so the team members can change course.

7 **Recognise them**. Professionals have pride. Feed their egos – praise good work in public and never, ever demean them in public. Have the hard conversations in private.

8 **Delegate**. If in doubt, delegate everything. Do not let the team delegate problems back up to you. Coach them to solve the problem themselves – they will learn and be more valuable team members as a result.

9 **Set expectations**. Some professionals want it all and want it now. Some want more and sooner. Any half comment about bonus and promotion will be taken as a 100% firm promise. Be clear and consistent in your messaging.

10 **Manage less**. Trust your team. Manage by walking away. Micro managing shows lack of trust and builds resentment among professionals. Trust your team and they will rise to the challenge.

If this is how you lead your professionals, it should also be how you lead all your staff. Just because someone does not have a string of degrees or professional qualifications to their name, that does not make them a second-class citizen. Most people want to have pride in what they do and want to do a good job. Treat them accordingly.

Chapter 20

Dealing with difficult people

To lead is to discover the full range of human nature. Some people make leadership a pleasure, others make it a challenge. Either way, leaders have to deal with it. As leaders, we should ensure we have the right team working for us. But while we cannot guarantee that our peers will be a pleasure to work with, we still have to work with them, knowing that we cannot change them. Ineffective leaders complain about awkward peer groups; effective leaders find ways of working with even the most awkward peer group.

> Effective leaders find ways of working with even the most awkward peer group.

Peer group dysfunction comes in a cornucopia of different flavours. Everyone has their own horror stories of colleagues from hell. To simplify things, most of the awkward types typically have one or more of the following five characteristics:

1 **Victims**. 'Poor me' people who believe the world treats them unfairly and that they are powerless to control a cruel universe.

2 **Villains**. Competitive politicians who always seek to undermine peers, spread blame when things go wrong and claim credit when things go well.

3 **Control freaks**. They believe in 'my way or no way'. Often found in staff departments using policies and procedure as a substitute for judgement, teamwork or sanity. For them, teamwork means doing what you are told, or you are not a team player.

4 **Indecisive types**. They wait in vain for the perfect, risk-free answer and then panic and make a decision which they then change, adapt or reverse. They are also often evasive and go missing when you most need them.

5 **Incompetents**. They may talk a good talk, but cannot actually do anything. When things go wrong they confuse matters with the 'I said/he said/she said/they said/I said' discussion.

Each horror story unfolds in its own unique and messy way and needs a unique response. However, there are a few principles to help you decide how to respond and how to help the awkward type spread their poison elsewhere. The principles are based on a range of rational, emotional and political responses that can be applied to all members of the awkward squad.

Rational response: stay action focused

Awkward squad members often enjoy discussing the past (what went wrong, why the world is unfair) and what is not possible (because of all our rules and procedures). These are unhelpful discussions: do not indulge them. Be clear about why you are having the discussion with them and what actions need to happen. Awkward types may push back by arguing that your idea should not happen or does not have priority. Be prepared for this. Initially, explain why you need to move forward. Then push the problem back onto the awkward squad member – ask them what options and alternatives they see. Try to create options rather than a take-it-or-leave-it choice which becomes a win/lose discussion. All the time you should be focusing on:

● the future, not the past

● actions, not analysis or behaviour

- win/win, not lose/lose
- options and discussion, not argument.

Emotional response: be positive with them and with yourself

One way to make the awkward squad happy is to indulge their behaviour, either by condoning it or by challenging it. If you condone it by sympathising, you reinforce their view that they can behave that way with you. If you challenge them, you open up a battle which, even if you are right rationally, you will lose politically and emotionally because you will have created an enemy. Simply ignore their behaviour – stay positive with your language and action focused with your discussion. Focus on the task, not on the behaviour. You are a leader, not a personal psychologist.

The awkward squad are often happiest when they are spreading their misery to everyone else. It is tempting to take their affronts personally, especially when they are meant personally. To do that is to hand them victory. Detach yourself and your emotions from their behaviour – observe their behaviour but do not become caught up in it. Remain focused on the task and remain positive. Although it is sometimes hard to believe, we are responsible for our own emotions – we can choose to feel happy, bored, angry or frustrated. We do not have to have our feelings dictated to us by the behaviour of others. If you ever want revenge on the awkward types, remember that happiness is the greatest revenge: if you have that, you have everything and they have nothing.

> Remain focused on the task and remain positive.

As you frame your emotional response, think about how a role model you admire would handle the situation. If your role model is a combination of Rambo, Darth Vader and Attila the Hun, you may want to choose a more positive role model – perhaps a peer or senior executive who seems to handle people well. Ultimately, you should aim to be a role model as well – behave as you would have others behave to you and behave in a way that commands respect in the organisation. In most workplaces, you will not advance by role modelling the behaviour of the awkward squad. The principles to follow are:

● remain positive and professional personally

● focus on the task, not behaviour: do not condone or challenge it.

Eventually, the awkward squad will find easier targets for them to be awkward with. The problem may remain, but it will no longer be your problem.

How to stay cool when the heat is on

Here are ten ways in which coachees have told me they stay cool when the heat is on. They vary from the sublime to the ridiculous. It does not matter what trick you have to keep cool as long as you have a trick that works for you.

1   Visualise the end of the event

Where do you want to be? Focus on that. Do not get caught up in the heat of battle. Stay calm and focused on where you want to get to.

2   Win a friend, not an argument

Arguing the moral righteousness of your position gets you nowhere. Fighting emotion with logic is like fighting fire with fuel: spectacular but not advisable.

3   Let the other side vent

Let them dump their emotion, let them be heard. No one can sustain fury for long. They cannot listen when they are angry. Having dumped, most people feel embarrassed. At least they can then talk sensibly.

4   Stay positive and constructive

You will be remembered more for how you behaved than for what you did. Leave the right impression; your behaviour may also persuade the other party to start being constructive.

▶

5   Imagine what your favourite role model would do in this situation, then do the same thing

If your role model is a mix of Darth Vader and Vlad the Impaler, do not use this technique.

6   Become a fly on the wall and watch the event

As you detach, you will be able to think more clearly and objectively, without getting emotionally involved.

7   Imagine Mr Nasty in a pink tutu

It is hard to get angry with a fat 50 year old in a pink tutu. Not laughing (or being sick) may be a greater challenge than staying calm.

8   Remember you have a choice.

You can be angry and upset or positive and professional. It's your choice: choose well.

9   Count to 10, just like your gran told you to

Let the immediate flush of anger pass and regain control of your feelings.

10   Breathe deeply, as taught in Buddhist meditation lessons

Like counting to 10, this allows you to regain control and lets you respond professionally.

Political response: engage your network

The awkward squad are not just awkward personally, they can also be awkward for your career – they may take pleasure in delaying or obstructing your plans, and may be happy quietly to spread poison about you. You have to deal with this. You need to deal with it carefully so that you are not contaminated by the poison. There are private and public ways of working the politics.

Ideally, you should be able to resolve matters directly with whoever is the cause of trouble. If dealing with them rationally, and with good emotional intelligence, does not work, you will need to move to a second line of defence: take advice in private from a trusted coach or mentor, but preferably not your boss. Your boss wants you to handle this sort of challenge yourself and does not want to get involved or pull rank unless absolutely necessary. As you take advice, take care: do not be negative about the awkward squad member. Focus on what needs to happen and what is stopping progress. Assume that anything you say will be repeated to the awkward squad member. The chances are that your coach will know what the individual is like anyway and will not need further briefing about their dysfunctional behaviour.

> **Focus on what needs to happen and what is stopping progress.**

The final line of defence is to find someone who can exert influence over the individual. The most obvious route is to escalate the matter to their boss. This may work in the short term but at the cost of creating a career enemy – no one likes finding that they have been short-circuited. Use this approach only if absolutely necessary.

Avoid letting your dispute go public. Even if you win, you will be damaged in the process. Keeping the email trail to 'prove' that you are right will not help. No boss wants to turn sleuth and figure out who wrote what when. The boss will want to end the dispute rather than apportion blame.

Chapter 21
Difficult conversations

No one likes difficult conversations. That means they are often avoided and problems are allowed to fester. If you are lucky, the problem solves itself. More often, the problem gradually gets worse and the tough conversation becomes even tougher. Leaders cannot live on easy street all the time – you have to deal with the tough stuff promptly and well.

The box here gives you ten tips for turning a difficult conversation into a productive conversation.

The art of the difficult conversation

1 **Know your goal**

   Know what you want to achieve by having the discussion. You should have a future-focused outcome: what will be different and better as a result of the conversation? Venting your anger, telling someone off or expressing your righteous indignation may make you feel better, but it will not improve your relationship, nor will it improve performance.

2 **Prepare**

   Understand the situation as best you can: find the right data or perspectives from colleagues. Many difficult conversations are made harder by misunderstandings, so remove them before you start. Then make sure you have the conversation at the right time and place. The right time is near the event so that memories are fresh, but not so close that emotions are still running high. Find the right place, which is always in private – that means just two of you. As soon as there is a third person, it is a public meeting and everyone will take public positions.

3   State the issue and your goal

The hardest part of the conversation is starting it. Be clear and to the point, and make sure you have a constructive goal. For instance: 'Our key customer reacted very badly in the last meeting. Let's discuss how we can deal with that and get a better reaction in future.' Avoid: 'You let the customer down badly, we need to discuss it', which has no positive outcome and is a conversation set up for conflict.

4   Seek to understand

Avoid misunderstandings. Start with questions. Open questions earn rich answers, such as 'Tell me what happened, tell me how you saw it'. You may also need to establish that there really is a problem, so 'Tell me what you wanted to achieve in that meeting'. You may need to push harder with a closed question: 'Is that the outcome you really wanted?'

5   Stick to the point

Tough conversations can be made tougher when the other person uses denial ('There was no problem') or distraction (raising other issues and agendas) or starts a debating club (the 'I said/she said/but he didn't anyway/I meant/and they wouldn't/so why didn't you' discussion). The point is you want to drive to a future-focused goal: keep sticking to that and allow no deviation.

6   Stay respectful

Never demean anyone, especially in a tense situation. Do not let emotion get into it. If someone does become emotional, even teary eyed, take a break and let them calm down. This allows for a more rational and productive discussion. It also prevents later claims of harassment.

7   Check yourself

Watch your language, your tone and your body language. Avoid being defensive, aggressive or emotional: the difficult conversation will then become impossible. Have some clear time before the meeting so that you can start it calmly and professionally and so that you are fully prepared for the meeting.

8   **Solve the problem together**
    If you have a brilliant solution in your mind, do not offer it. Instead, ask them what they would do. There is a risk they may come up with an even better solution. If it is their solution, they will be committed to making it work. If you foist your solution on them, they will be committed to showing it is a dumb idea that does not work.

9   **Check agreement**
    A classic mistake is to end the meeting when you both sound happy, without confirming what you have agreed. Then it all unravels when you find you left with different understandings. End by asking them what they think happens next. If they say what you expect, you have an agreement. If they tell you something unexpected, or more likely incomplete and evasive, you know you have more work to do.

10 **Have the conversation**
    This is the most important point. Do not duck the conversation and do not delegate the problem upwards or sideways to colleagues. These conversations are never perfect, but the more often you have them, the better you become at making them productive.

Not all difficult conversations are open ended. If you have bad news to give about pay, bonus, promotions, assignments or job prospects, then it is pointless to start a fake open discussion. You still need to prepare, stay respectful and check yourself, but you need to come to the point fast and deliver the bad news directly. Avoid long explanations or discussion – that will simply fog the issue and is an invitation to bargaining and pleading. Only once the decision has been understood and accepted can you move onto any explanation or next steps as appropriate.

> You need to come to the point fast and deliver the bad news directly.

If you want to lead, you have to deal with the tough stuff. The good news is that the more often you do it, the easier it is and the better you deal with it.

Chapter 22

Firing people

'Firing' is a dirty word. The corporate jargon is full of euphemisms which avoid the awkward reality that when you fire someone you seriously mess with their lives. Instead, we hear sanitised words such as rightsizing, downsizing, offshoring, best shoring, outsourcing, laying off, redeploying and letting go. It sounds clean and reasonable, unless you are on the wrong end of the action. In reality, most leaders know that they are damaging people's lives and they would prefer to avoid the messy reality of making these tough decisions.

Ultimately, your responsibility is to your organisation: the survival of the organisation takes precedence over the survival of the individual. Having the wrong person in the wrong place puts many other jobs at risk. You have to make the difficult decision and change people who are not in the right post. But this also means that your firing decision must be seen to be right and fair, not just a personal vendetta. Fair process is essential to maintaining morale.

> The survival of the organisation takes precedence over the survival of the individual.

Firing people assumes you know when it is right to fire someone. There are plenty of poor reasons for firing people which I have seen:

- needing a scapegoat when things go wrong
- pursuing a personal vendetta

- making a statement about your power as the new boss
- punishing a one-off failure or setback
- making room to promote a favourite
- eliminating a potential rival.

All of these reasons get noticed in the organisation, even when they are denied. They breed a culture of politics, mistrust and fear, which are not good starting points for a high-performing team.

You need to know how to read genuine distress signals around individual performance. Failing to meet numbers or any other underperformance is not necessarily a distress signal: there are many legitimate reasons why a setback might occur. Few leaders can claim to have never had a setback. The task is to differentiate between a one-off problem and a pattern of failure.

> Few leaders can claim to have never had a setback.

The typical career death spiral has some classic patterns:

- repeated failure to meet deadlines or goals, followed by pleading to change deadlines or goals and denial that they were fair, achievable or clear in the first place
- failure to take responsibility: blaming others
- unclear communication leading to a 'he said/I said/she said/I said/they said' discussion when things go wrong
- becoming invisible: in its final stages often marked by increasing sick leave and other absences from the office
- increasingly direct complaints from colleagues.

In contrast, someone who has a setback but takes responsibility, communicates clearly, maintains visibility and sorts out the problem is more likely to be a success than a failure. But when the death spiral is set in motion, there is rarely a way back for the individual. You need to move fast and put everyone out of their misery.

Chapter 23

Build influence across your organisation

anagement used to be about making things happen through other people. In the twenty-first century, management has become more interesting and more challenging. It is now about making things happen through people you do not control, and you may not even like. In the old world, managers controlled the resources they needed to make things happen. In an era of flat organisations and outsourced work, managers no longer have control over the resources they need to succeed. The leadership challenge steps up the management challenge: leaders have to take people they do not control to where they would not have got by themselves.

> Leaders have to take people they do not control to where they would not have got by themselves.

So how can you exercise influence over people you do not control? The simplistic answer is that you can exert indirect control through money or referred authority. Money is self-explanatory: if you have the budget, then you can commission services from people you do not formally control. Referred authority is where you refer to the authority of a boss higher up the food chain: the big boss wants this, so you have to comply. Variations of this are played by technical specialists: you have to do this because health and safety, legal or HR say you have to do it. Money and referred authority work in the short term – you gain compliance – but you do not gain commitment.

There are limits to how far you can play the referred authority game. It causes resentment and eventually people bite back. Equally, you will not have an unlimited pot of money with which to buy influence. So you need to find other ways of building and sustaining influence across and beyond your own sphere of control.

You have two tools to build your influence: first, you need a clear and relevant agenda; second, you need to build trust with people who matter. We have already encountered the importance of having an agenda when it comes to taking control of your unit. The same message applies when building influence more widely: you need a clear agenda.

If no one knows what you are doing, you will be ignored. If you are driving a programme that has importance and relevance across the organisation, no one will ignore you. A clear agenda helps you in at least four ways because it:

- gives you visibility beyond your own unit
- enables you to decide which battles to fight and which to avoid
- tells you who you need to influence and bring on board
- helps you focus on your real priorities.

If you turn this around, lack of a clear and relevant agenda means you become invisible, you don't know which battles are worth fighting, you don't know who to influence or what your main priorities should be. Clarity counts. Relevance also matters. Relevance in this case begs the question: who is my agenda relevant to? If it is relevant to the janitor, you may have a grateful janitor to work with. If it is relevant to the CEO and board, you will suddenly find the machinery of your business grinds into action to support your agenda. Choose your agenda well.

If you have money, an agenda and referred power, you can gain compliance. Essentially you enter into a series of transactions with your colleagues, where you can use these tools to get your way. However, there are many occasions when these tools will not be at your disposal. At these times you cannot force compliance. You need to gain other people's willing support. You have to be the leader people want to follow, rather than the leader people have to follow.

> You have to be the leader people want to follow, rather than the leader people have to follow.

This is where trust becomes important. Is there anyone you have wanted to work for who you do not trust? You may have had to work for people you do not trust, that is the way of life, but few people would choose to do so.

Once you have trust, you move from winning your way in a series of transactions to having a relationship that can be productive even in hard times. So how do you become the trusted leader and how do you build trust? You could try saying things like this:

- 'OK, John, I'm a straight sort of guy … be kind to me … of course I'm an honest sort of a bloke.'
- 'I think most people who have dealt with me think I am a pretty straight sort of guy, and I am.'

The first case was Prime Minister Tony Blair discussing his role in the Iraq war; in the second he was discussing his decision to accept donations from the boss of Formula One (both on the BBC). Whatever the merits of each case, claiming to be honest and trustworthy is probably the best way to appear dishonest and untrustworthy. You cannot demand trust, you have to deserve trust.

There is a simple way of thinking about trust, which is captured in a formula. Here it is:

$$T = \frac{C \times I}{R}$$

where:

T = trust
C = credibility
I = intimacy
R = risk

Forget the spurious mathematical accuracy implied by the formula. What it says is that people trust you the more you can show intimacy (you have common interests, needs or values) and credibility (you do what you say). But trust decreases with risk.

We will see how you can use each element to build trust.

Risk

Trust is not an on–off switch. Our trust rises or falls with the level of risk. You may trust a stranger to give you directions to the nearest post office; you would be unwise to trust a stranger on the street with your life savings. This is a simple and obvious insight which we can put to use where we work.

Start by accepting that trust is incremental. When you first start at a new place of work, no one really knows you. You have to prove yourself step by step. And that is how it is with trust. Do not ask too much of people too soon: show that you can be trusted on the small things and slowly they will start to trust you on the bigger things as well.

You can also try to de-risk ideas and proposals. Many ideas are killed not because they are bad ideas but because they are seen to be risky. So remove the risk – ask approval for just the first phase; demonstrate it is not risky by reference to similar ideas that have succeeded; remove the personal and political risk by showing that the idea has the support of other key people.

Intimacy

There is a long and ignoble tradition of using personal intimacy to secure advancement. Although that approach can be successful, it is not what is meant by intimacy in this context. Intimacy is something we can all practise if we want to build trust. It is about showing that you have the same values, interests or needs as the person you are with. This means it is worth taking time to research people before you meet them: Facebook, Google and mutual colleagues are mines of information. You should be able to find something you have in common.

When you see people meeting for the first time, they often appear to waste the initial minutes talking about nothing very much. The apparently random chit chat about places they have worked, people they have worked with is an attempt to find common ground and shared experience.

The need for intimacy is the enemy of diversity. We trust people like ourselves, because we assume that we know how they think. The result can be to hire and promote people on the basis of who they are and where they were educated, instead of on the basis of merit. If you come from a different background to the people you work with, you have to work hard to establish the bonds of common interest.

> There is one other secret weapon you can deploy to build trust: listen.

As we have already seen, there is one other secret weapon you can deploy to build trust: listen. The more you listen, the more you learn. The act of listening is a form of flattery – we are always pleased when someone else appears interested in our triumphs and travails, however trivial they may be.

Credibility

If intimacy is about saying the right things, credibility is about doing as you say. In the popular jargon, you have to 'walk the talk'.

We all like to think that we do as we say. The problem is not that we are all devious – most of us do not set out to deceive or to let people down – but that we land up letting colleagues down for two reasons. First, events conspire against us. In the words of the proverb, the road to hell is paved with good intentions. But then life intervenes. Priorities change; a supplier lets us down; the IT system crashes; there was transport chaos. There are always reasons why it may not be possible to do as you say. We know we have a perfectly good reason why we could not do as we said. All your colleague knows is that you did not do as you said. We all have colleagues who are very good at producing excuses: they are not the colleagues we trust. If something is important, make it happen. When you accept excuses, you accept failure.

There is a second, more pernicious way in which we find we do not do as we say. The problem is not in our actions, it is in our words. What we say and what is heard are often very different. People hear what they want to hear, so take care in what you say. For instance, we may tell a customer that we will do our best to get the delivery on time. When the delivery is late we say we did our best as promised. What the customer was expecting was an on-time delivery, so we failed and lost credibility. If you tell a team member that you will put them up for promotion and they do not get it, then you can show that you did as you said: you put them up for promotion. What the team member was expecting was that you would secure their promotion and you failed. You have just lost credibility and trust.

> People hear what they want to hear, so take care in what you say.

We can complain that we have been misinterpreted, but that misses the point. As a leader, it is our job to make sure we are not misunderstood. We have to communicate clearly and set expectations clearly. If in doubt, set expectations low. This is a trick we have all learned when dealing with bosses: under-promise and over-deliver. It is a good principle in dealing with anyone. So if there is any doubt about securing a promotion for your team member, paint a picture that shows that promotion is close to impossible but you will try anyway. Then keep on reinforcing the message.

The importance of credibility is hard to overstate. If you are not seen as reliable, you will not be trusted. It is as simple as that. Even one failure to deliver is toxic – it can undo all the hard work you have put in on making other things happen. No one will remember all the times you did as you said, they will remember the one time you let them down. You can remember, probably vividly, when you have been let down and you will remember who let you down. Don't become one of those people. Credibility is like a vase: when you break it, it is very hard to put back together.

Popularity?

There is one dead end in building influence across the organisation: popularity. Leadership is not a popularity contest, outside politics. We can learn from politics about why leadership is not a popularity contest. The more you seek popularity, the weaker and less trustworthy you become. Instead of making hard and unpopular decisions, the popular leader seeks an easy way out. Even worse, weak leaders make promises to attract support. When these promises cannot be delivered, trust plummets. It is no surprise to find that politicians are among the least trusted professionals: we have all grown used to hearing promises which are not then delivered. The politicians will then quote back at us their weasel words which show that they did not actually promise what we expected – they will say it was not a promise, it was an aspiration or a hope or a target. But they did not promise. In doing so, they also show the importance of setting expectations very clearly from the start if we want to be trusted as opposed to popular.

Chapter 24

Manage your boss

Most of the management literature focuses on how leaders should manage their teams. This omits the most important person in a leader's work: their boss. Leaders have bosses. Leadership is not about your title, it is about what you do. If you are a true leader, leading from the middle of the organisation you may have more than one boss. Even if you are the CEO, you will have to report to a board and a chair person. And if you want to be effective, you have to manage your boss well – they have the power to make life good or bad for you.

In practice, most of us spend more time trying to work out how to manage our boss than we do trying to work out how to manage each team member. This is rational. Our boss is more important to our wellbeing and career survival than any one team member. You may rest assured that your team members also invest great effort in working out how they can manage you.

> Learning to manage your boss is a good test of your leadership skills.

Learning to manage your boss is a good test of your leadership skills: you have to learn to manage in the absence of formal control when the stakes are high. It is leadership without the safety net. If you can manage your boss well, then you can apply most of the lessons to managing your team and beyond.

In theory, you should be able to manage your boss by sitting down and having a formal exchange of expectations. This would set out performance expectations and the expected way of working on both sides. In theory, the world should be able to live in peace. Reality is far removed from theory. You have to take responsibility for managing this vital relationship, whatever your boss may be like.

There are three main principles to work on:

1 Adapt your style.

2 Build trust.

3 Have a plan B.

Adapt your style

You may or may not like your boss's style. But you can be sure that your boss will not change their style to suit you. If you dislike your boss, that is your problem. If your boss dislikes you or your style, that is also your problem. One way or the other, you have to find a way of working with your boss's style. That does not mean you ape your boss – if your boss is a psychopath, there is no point in trying to become a psychopath yourself.

Your boss does not come with a user manual. You have to work out the rules for yourself and then act accordingly. For instance, if your boss is best first thing in the morning but you like a lie-in, you have a choice to make: lie in or work well with the boss. If your boss uses deductive thinking (working from principles to action), you could drive them to distraction by sticking with inductive reasoning (working from evidence to conclusions). Your ways of thinking might balance each other and could be highly productive, but you would need to communicate your thinking in a way that resonates with your boss.

Clashes between bosses and team members are often about style, but are disguised as 'performance problems' by the boss. If the two of you clash over style, then the boss will start thinking about you differently. Most of the time, bosses want to be supportive – you are presumed to be innocent and events are interpreted accordingly. But if there is a culture clash, the presumption of innocence can quickly become a presumption of guilt: the boss will interpret events negatively. Your triumphs will be dismissed and any setbacks will be magnified and assumed to be your fault. This soon becomes a completely untenable position. You have to perform, but you also have to adapt to your boss's style.

Build trust

We have already looked at the trust equation:

$$T = \frac{C \times I}{R}$$

The same principles apply to working with your boss, but with three twists:

- **Intimacy**: this is more than just showing you share your boss's values and priorities, this is about loyalty. In practice, most leaders tolerate incompetence far longer than they tolerate disloyalty. Most mistakes are forgivable, but disloyalty is not. Disloyalty is not just about actively sabotaging your boss, it is as simple as failing to speak up when your boss needs support, upstaging or outshining them, or blaming them in public.

- **Credibility**: ultimately, you have to perform. If you have a gold medal in incompetence, then no matter how much the boss likes you, you will go. That means you have to have difficult conversations with your boss as soon as possible. If your boss offers you a project and you think you cannot do it in the timeframe suggested, have that conversation immediately. Do not come back with excuses later and try to renegotiate. If a project is going awry, let your boss know early so that corrective action can be taken. This can be hard with some bosses who

preach 'Don't bring me problems, bring me solutions: are you
a solutions person or a problems person?' This was the culture
at RBS before the crash: no one dared to flag up the problems
with bad debts until the lid blew off the toxic mess and the
taxpayer had to bail out the bank. Credibility is about setting
expectations, as well as delivering against those expectations.

● **Risk**: bosses hate surprises and not just because surprises are
rarely good ones. The problem with a surprise is that it shows
that the boss is not in control, and that is very damaging for
your boss. Help your boss look in control at all times. This
is more than just project updates. It is also about sharing
information: bosses hate it when they are embarrassed in front
of colleagues because they did not know something that you
knew about.

Have a plan B

Your plan A should be to work well with your boss. You need a plan
B for what happens if things do not go well with your boss.

Within Plan A, you need to know how you will make a difference.
One way you help your boss is by removing routine rubbish and
dealing with the day-to-day noise of
the organisation. You may not get
much credit for this, but if your boss
is sucked into such minutiae, you will
not be appreciated. If that is all you

> You need a claim to
> fame.

do, then you will be a worthy but minor part of the team – you will
not be seen as a leader. To lead, you need to find a project where
you can make a difference. You need a claim to fame. By definition,
this is likely to be hard and to be out of your comfort zone. It is the
sort of project where you will learn and grow fast. Go for it.

You also need a plan B. If you have no Plan B, you become
completely dependent on your boss. This is the fate of most PhD
students, who find they become a form of indentured labour to

their professor, on whom their entire future depends. Dependency is fine if you have a powerful boss who you can trust, is highly supportive and will not move when the next reorganisation comes along. Those conditions are highly unlikely to hold for long.

Plan B is tightly linked to building your network within and beyond your place of work. Within work, your network will tell you who the good bosses and projects are, and where the death star bosses and projects lurk. Do not leave yourself to the vagaries of the formal assignment system. Make yourself visible and useful to bosses and projects that interest you. When the death stars loom, don the Harry Potter cloak of invisibility: make sure you look overworked and indispensable in your current role. Keep your network beyond work live – you will know other people in your industry, some of whom you may have worked with in the past. If you need to make a rapid exit, your external network may be your safety net. Between 65% and 85% of jobs are landed through networking as opposed to advertising and headhunting.

> **Make yourself visible and useful to bosses and projects that interest you.**

As a coach, I hear many clients complain bitterly about their boss. Ultimately, you have to take responsibility for your career. You either have to adapt to your boss or find a boss you can work with. Complaining about your boss is therapeutic but ineffective.

Part 3

Action: make it happen

Introduction

The productivity of effective and less effective sales people is dramatic. For instance, MetLife found that its best insurance people were twice as effective as its least effective sales people. This is a normal finding in sales-related jobs, where it is easy to make productivity comparisons. Most professional jobs are much more ambiguous than sales: success is less clear and depends on quality as much as quantity. Comparing productivity across professionals is much harder because no one is doing quite the same job. If anything, this means that productivity variations between professionals are likely to be even greater than between sales people. Bluntly, it is easier for anyone with an ambiguous workload to hide, whereas there is no hiding place for sales people. This resonates with experience. In your workplace you probably know who really makes things happen and who hides. The productivity gap between the best and the worst can be fourfold or more, even though it is hard to prove.

So what does it take to be in the high-performance group when it comes to making things happen? You have three priorities:

1 **Be very clear about your goals and priorities**. Know what you want to achieve. If you do not know what you want, you are unlikely to find it. Goal focus lets you separate out the noise of day-to-day management from the signal. Deal with the noise, but create time to make progress towards your goal. This should sound familiar: it is about having a clear Idea as part of your IPA agenda.

2 **Find help**. You cannot do it all alone, so build a team that will help you succeed. Build a network of influence and support across your organisation that will also help you. Again, this will sound familiar: it is the People part of your IPA agenda. With a great idea and great people, you are well on the way to making it happen.

3   **Master your craft**. This is where you can personally make a difference – and they are the things all leaders deal with. This is the focus of the remainder of this book.

Already, you will be mastering some technical skills in operations, finance, law or whatever your chosen area of expertise may be. As a leader you need to master three more sorts of skills which this part of the book will explore:

1   **Organisational skills**. As a leader, you have to know how to lead change, make projects work, control costs, deal with budgets, handle crises and conflicts, and make and influence decisions in uncertainty. Any one of these skills can take years to master, but the basic principles are fairly simple and they are laid out in the chapters that follow.

2   **Personal skills**. If you have to explain to a five year old what you do all day, then explaining how you manage the intricacies of a global supply chain will not get you far. But if you say you meet, talk and listen to people, and read and write papers, you may be understood. That is the mundane reality of what leaders actually do all day, but some are very good at it and others are not. Hone these daily skills and you will stand out from your peers.

3   **Mindset skills**. The best leaders act differently because they think differently. If there is an X-factor to great leadership, it is here. Fortunately, research is showing that the way the best leaders think is consistent, predictable and can be learned by anyone. This part of the book closes by reviewing this leading-edge research and showing how you can build your own version of the X-factor.

Part 3 of the book starts with organisational skills because these are the bread and butter of making things happen.

Chapter 25
Managing change

Leadership is about taking people where they would not have got by themselves. That means that change is at the heart of leadership. It is not enough for a leader to simply maintain or improve things – that is what any manager should do and it is very hard work – a leader will make a difference by changing how things work and moving towards a new future perfect.

In theory, we should all like change. Change is what brings about progress and prosperity: new technologies and greater efficiencies that link the global economy. In practice, we like it when other people and firms change, which will benefit us. When we have to change, suddenly change becomes a lot less attractive. Change is no longer about opportunity, it is about risk. Change means changing how we work, perhaps who we work for, and where we work and what we do. We have to learn new rules of survival and success, which may or may not be good for us. The greater the change, the greater the perceived risk and the greater the passive and active resistance becomes.

> If you want to make real change, you will face real resistance.

So if you want to make real change, you will face real resistance. This alters the definition of leadership from 'taking people where they would not have got by themselves' to 'taking people where they do not want to go (to start with)'.

> Change means
> personal change
> and that makes the
> change process highly
> emotional.

The great mistake in contemplating change is to think about it as a rational process, which can be captured in neat Gantt or PERT charts. The reality is different. Change means personal change and that makes the change process highly emotional. Change also means changing the organisation – changes in the pecking order mean that change is also a highly political process.

If you want to make change work, you have to manage the change process on three levels:

1 Rational.

2 Political.

3 Emotional.

The assiduous project manager will work in the rational world of the project. As a change leader you have to work with the political and emotional agendas of colleagues to effect change and to assure the success of diverse projects. 'Working the political and emotional agendas' sounds vague and slightly undoable. Much of it comes down to experience, which does not help much if you do not have the experience. Even if you do have the experience, it pays to have something more structured than your innate genius and intuition to rely on when it comes to making change. What worked last time may not work in different circumstances this time.

In practice, there are three tools that can help you maximise the chances of success in dealing with change:

1 Setting up change to succeed.

2 Managing the change process.

3 Managing the change network.

Setting up change to succeed

Most sane people do not enjoy change. Change implies uncertainty and risk. Even if I can succeed currently, how do I know that I can succeed in a new environment with a new boss doing new things? The less control over the change I have, the more I am likely to fear it. So change is dominated by the **FUD** factor:

Fear
Uncertainty
Doubt

The only people who do not suffer from the FUD factor are CEOs, senior leaders and consultants. They are able to control the change and they know how they intend to benefit from it.

In practice, most change programmes succeed or fail before they even start. As a leader, your crucial role is to make sure that change is set up for success, not failure. You may think this takes too much time, but it is time well invested to assure success. Over the years, one simple formula has been a constant predictor of change success or failure. Here it is, in all its spurious mathematical accuracy:

$$\mathbf{V + N + C + F} \geq \mathbf{R}$$

V = Vision

This is not a 'save the planet' type vision. This is your future perfect idea. Show how your unit, firm or organisation is going to be different and better as a result of the change. This is your Idea of the IPA agenda. To make the vision compelling, make it relevant to each person. Show how they have a role to play in the change and how they will benefit from the change.

N = Need

There has to be a perceived need to change, both for the institution and for the individual. Show that the risks of doing nothing must outweigh the risks of doing something. Fear is often a powerful motivator for change. Increasing the fear of inaction is effective although unkind. CEOs often do this by creating a 'burning platform'. Essentially, they argue that if there is no change, then the firm will be put out of business by competition, regulators or technology. The risk of change suddenly becomes low compared with the risk of losing your job.

C = Capacity to change

It is no use having both the vision and the need if the organisation lacks the skills or resources to change. Your team wants to know that they can make the journey from today to tomorrow successfully. Your capacity to change rests on two pillars. First, you need the resources to make it happen: you need the budget, team and top management support for it. Second, you need credibility. If a new change initiative is announced every six months and forgotten three months later, your latest initiative will be politely ignored. Demonstrate that this change is for real, which brings us on to first steps.

F = First steps

We live in a world of instant gratification. We want to know that we are backing a winner. Use this to your advantage. Seek out some early wins – some early signs of success that will bring all the doubters and fence-sitters on board. Create a sense of excitement; trumpet any progress loudly so that you appear to be at the head of a bandwagon. Let others join your bandwagon.

R = Risks and costs of change

The risks of change are normally dealt with by the standard corporate infrastructure of risk logs, issue logs and mitigating actions. These are useful in a limited way. They deal with the rational risks of change, which most managers are comfortable with. But the real risks of change are not rational, they are emotional and political. The emotional risks are about individuals who feel threatened by change. The political risks come from challenging the status quo, threatening the status of other units and generally disrupting the organisation.

Emotional and political obstacles are hard to spot. Normally they are hidden behind a whole raft of rational objections to change such as 'This will cost too much' or 'Customers will hate it'. These are camouflage for the real risks, which are 'I feel threatened by this' and 'My unit is threatened by this'. If you deal with the rational objection, you miss the point and simply get stuck in an irrelevant and unwinnable debate. Take time out in private with each individual to understand and deal with their real agenda, and you will find that the rational objections mysteriously disappear of their own accord.

As a leader, it pays to work the whole agenda. Constantly remind people of the vision and relate it to their needs. Build up the need to change and the risks of doing nothing. Find some early successes to keep people encouraged and make sure that there is enough capacity to support the change. All of this needs to be balanced against risk reduction: few people truly enjoy risk. The greater the perceived risk, the greater the resistance to change. Make the change very low risk and no one will get in your way.

> Build up the need to change and the risks of doing nothing.

Managing the change process

Project managers can manage the technical and rational aspects of change. As a change leader you must manage the political and emotional consequences of change. Most significant change programmes go through a predictable emotional and political cycle, outlined in Figure 25.1.

If you have used the change equation successfully, then there will be some early enthusiasm for change. Some early wins bring more of the doubters on board and everything starts to look good. It is at this point that things start to go wrong. After the initial flush of enthusiasm dies away, slowly people start to understand the scale of the change required. They start to see the logical consequences

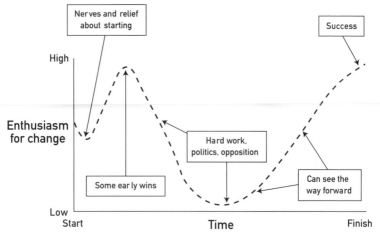

Figure 25.1 Change and the valley of death

of change; the exciting vision of the change you painted becomes obscured by the reality of the effort and risks involved.

There is rarely one event that triggers collapse. Usually the change slowly meanders into a swamp of despair. The fair-weather friends who hopped on board at the first sign of success are hopping off at the first sign of trouble. They now create distance between themselves and your change. They may offer advice, but it is poisoned advice. Take their advice and then they will claim they turned the programme around. Refuse the advice and they will have the ammunition to show that you failed because you refused the advice. Suddenly, you can start to feel very lonely and very beleaguered.

Inevitably, prevention is better than cure for the mid-life crises of change. If you have put in the right preconditions for success, in terms of both project management and the change agenda, you will pull through. If the change was started prematurely, you may fail. There will not be enough belief in the vision or enough political support to overcome the opposition to change.

Curiously, the valley of death is essential to most successful change programmes. It is only in the valley of death that people fully realise the scale of the change they will need to make. Opposition to change is the surest sign that they are at last taking the change seriously, that they are engaged. Do not avoid the valley of death: seek it out.

In most major changes I have started, I have alerted the client or the sponsor to the change cycle and the valley of death at the start. If they know it is coming, they worry about it less, they realise it is natural and are ready to work through it. In several cases the CEO has kept on asking, like a child on a long journey, 'Are we there yet? Is this it? Have we got to the valley of death yet?' The valley of death experience is uncomfortable but important. It is the moment when everyone realises that they can no longer continue with the old ways, even if they do not yet know what the future holds. This is when everyone is really grasping reality and is ready to move on.

> Leaders look to the future: keep your eyes fixed on the end goal and figure out the way of getting there.

In the valley of death, followers give up. Leaders look to the future: keep your eyes fixed on the end goal and figure out the way of getting there. At a time when everyone else is seeing problems, you will stand out by offering solutions and actions. In this slough of despondency, people want solutions. The valley of death is your moment of truth, it is when you prove your capability and it will be when you learn and develop the most.

If all this does is to give you some hope next time your change effort hits crisis, then it has at least done some good. Remember, the difference between success and failure is often no more than persistence.

Managing the change network

There is one big catch in setting up change to succeed. Leaders often want everyone to join their jolly bandwagon. Normally, this is not possible. There will always be some diehards who would resist anything. The successful change network consists of those people who collectively have the power, skills and resources to assure the success of the change. In addition, the change leader needs the critical mass of the organisation to be supportive. It is a trap to try to engage the whole organisation. The challenge can be seen in Figure 25.2.

This figure shows that most people feel pretty indifferent to the idea of change in principle. In practice, their enthusiasm will wax and wane depending on where they are in the valley of death. But the bell curve effect will always be present.

There are always extremes at each end of the change bell curve. At one end are the change enthusiasts whom you can recruit as the active leaders and early adopters of change. At the other end, some will always resist. Do not waste time on them. Let them see that

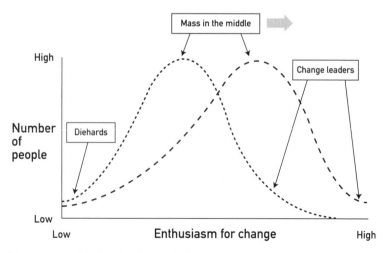

Figure 25.2 Shifting the change bell curve

the change is succeeding and allow them to make up their own minds. They will start to feel lonely, left on the platform after the change train moves off. They can decide to leave or get on board. If they want to protest by lying down on the tracks in front of the train, let them know the train will not stop anyway. The change resisters can consume a disproportionate amount of your time and effort. In practice, you need to move the mass of people from neutrality to mild acceptance of change. Again, do not expect everyone to become change enthusiasts.

Achieving critical mass

At one chemicals company, the plant manager was frustrated that he could not implement a new set of working practices. We were asked to help. We soon heard loud objections to the whole change idea, expressed very forcibly. They used every reason to object, from cost to work–life balance to health and safety to threats of walkouts. But we found the objections were all coming from a small group of staff and managers in the power plant. Most other people were quietly supportive, but felt overawed by the loud-mouthed middle managers. And the plant manager had let himself become hostage to them – they had secured an effective veto over his plans.

Instead of focusing on the objectors, we focused on the supporters. As we started to implement the changes in the more supportive areas, people realised they liked the changes and became bolder about supporting them. We did not need to negotiate with the objectors – one by one they made their own decisions. Some got with the programme, some got out. As a change leader, do not try to please all the people all the time, you will get nowhere.

Aside from the mass of people, you must build the right power network in support of change. Building networks and alliances is essential to your success in the middle of the matrix and is the subject of the next chapter.

Chapter 26

Managing projects

Project management versus change management

Change management and project management are the bread and butter of all leaders. Change and project management are often talked of as if they are the same thing. They are not. Project management is the technical, task-focused subset of change management. Projects focus on who does what, where, when and how. The art of leadership can be thought of as a series of linked projects which help people go where they would not have got by themselves.

If you are very senior, the art of project management is simple: you hire someone (or some consultants) to manage the project for you. But for most leaders, project management is a vital art to master if you are to make things happen. And if you do hire help to manage your project, you need to know enough to make sure they are doing their job well.

> Project management is a vital art to master if you are to make things happen.

Good project management is the hallmark of a good manager. The manager delivers against preordained goals with preordained resources. Good change management is the hallmark of the good leader. The leader goes beyond formal authority, using influencing and political skills effectively, to make things happen.

Project management or change management?

The contrast between change and project management became clear in a merger. The two sides of the merger brought in some consultants to help, which is always a dangerous idea. The partner did what the board needed, he acted as a leader. Although he had no formal authority, he convened the executive committee on a daily basis and helped them work through the daily crises that occur in any merger. Behind the scenes, he worked the politics of the individuals involved. The consultants then put in a team to project manage the merger integration. After ten days, they had established a war room with risk logs and issue logs, meeting logs, attendance logs, telephone logs and master logs. Everything was being logged and nothing was being done. The client went crazy. Logs and paper do not change things, people do. They tried to manage change; you have to lead change.

However, leaders also have to deliver the basics of project management. We will look at effective project management below.

The basics of project management

Good project management is a real skill and it is in short supply. Projects have a nasty habit of taking twice as long and costing twice as much as the original bid. Anyone who has had building work done knows this, to their cost. Some projects go completely out of control. The cost of building the Scottish Parliament escalated from an initial £10 million to £20 million bid to more than £400 million. The London Olympics cost three times the original estimate. Politicians may be great leaders, they are rarely good managers.

Here we will not focus on the vagaries of contract management. One reason contractors cost more than you thought is that they underbid in the first place. Either they were too optimistic, or they hoped to make up their loss on all the changes and additions that are inevitably requested in the course of any project, from building a new kitchen to delivering the London Olympics. For the buyer this is called a cost overrun, which is not good. For the supplier it is called income progression, which they rely on.

There are exhaustive manuals on how to run tight projects. We will focus on the few items that make the big difference. Most projects, like most battles and most change, are decided before they really start. It pays to make sure that your projects are set up for success, not failure.

Success depends on four basic principles:

1   The right problem.
2   The right sponsor.
3   The right team.
4   The right process.

Get these wrong and your project is doomed. Get them right and it takes a stroke of evil genius to make it go wrong. Figure 26.1 illustrates where, as a leader, you should focus your efforts: at the start, before the heavy lifting begins.

We will take a look at each of the four principles of success.

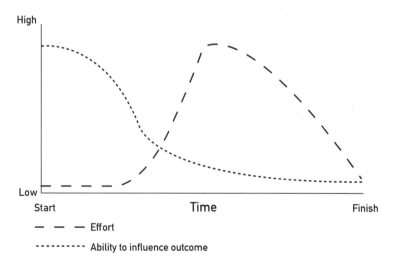

Figure 26.1 Projects: effort and ability to influence the outcome

The right problem

There is a story of a drunk who loses his house keys in a dark alley. He can't see anything there, so he goes into the main street where there is plenty of street lighting and looks for his house keys there. He figures that at least there he can see what he is looking for. Too many managers look where it is easy, not where it is useful. To be useful, we must look in the right area and solve the right problem, even when it is difficult.

> Too many managers look where it is easy, not where it is useful.

There are many experts who know the answer. They are like solutions drifting across the business world in search of a problem to which they can attach themselves. Their pitch is as beguiling as that of the quack doctors in the Wild West selling their miracle cure-all medicines. Because they offer an easy answer, often management leaps aboard the bandwagon. A good answer is useless if it answers the wrong problem. '42' is a good answer to 'What is six times seven?' It is also, for some people, a good answer to 'What is the meaning of life?' It is not such a good answer to 'What is the capital of Croatia?'

Finding the right problem is not easy. We are offered cost cutting, re-engineering, supply chain management, service excellence and all manner of initiatives. In all cases, repeatedly asking 'why' helps.

Finding the real problem

A hotel manager wanted to raise room rates. We started to ask why. We took a couple of weeks of digging around to find the data, which produced this logic flow:

We must raise room rates	Why?
Because we must improve profits	Why?

▶

Because profits are down	Why?
Because our costs per customer are up	Why?
Because we are getting fewer customers	Why?
Because competitors charge less than us	So ...
We should reduce room rates	

Naturally, the logic flow does not drop out quite as simply as that. It might take anything from a few minutes to a few months to tease out the logic flow. In this case, the logic flow encouraged the hotel manager to take exactly the opposite action from his first intention – he cut room rates instead of raising them.

The right sponsor

There is an easy way to find the right problem – find the right sponsor. Consultants love working for chief executives, for several reasons:

- You always get paid.
- The CEO has the power and authority to make things happen and can cut through political log-jams.
- A CEO project always succeeds. Even if it fails, it will still be made to look like a success in public.

If you are the CEO, this is very dangerous. You will find many people eager to please you by agreeing with you and putting your ideas into action. They will revel in using your proxy power: 'Do this because the boss wants it.' Fewer people take the risk to stand up and tell you that you are being daft. It is possible that the CEO is solving the wrong problem. There is often a conspiracy of silence that lets the CEO plough on in the wrong direction. Challenging the CEO is a dangerous sport. You may land up becoming highly trusted and valued for your insight and honesty. You may land up doing the corporate equivalent of cleaning toilets in Siberia.

Not all projects are CEO projects, but the same characteristics are required of a good sponsor:

- The project should be a 'must-win' battle for the future personal success of the sponsor. You want a sponsor who is totally committed to success. Otherwise, you suffer asymmetric risk: you take the risk of failure while the sponsor walks away, or the sponsor claims the credit if you succeed.

- The sponsor must have the power and influence to be able to overcome all the political log-jams that occur on any project.

- The sponsor has to have enough authority and resources to enable the project to happen.

The right team

Inevitably, the people you want on a project team are not available. If people are good, then they are fully committed elsewhere. The only people who are available are the people sitting on the beach, waiting to become fully utilised. They are typically a mix of the untried and untested, together with a few who have been tried and tested and have not covered themselves in glory. Even if some good people are available, they may well not have the particular technical skills that are important for the success of your project. As we have seen in the second part of the book, make sure you recruit people with the right values. Projects rarely go smoothly and you will need people with resilience, creativity and initiative to help you through the tough patches.

> You will need people with resilience, creativity and initiative to help you through the tough patches.

At this point, the successful project manager should play hardball. Accepting the B team is a recipe for B-grade results, long nights, crises and frustration. A good way of testing how important a project is is to see who is placed on the project team. If the sponsor and CEO are happy to see a B team on the project, they clearly regard it as a B-type priority. This is a good time to walk away from the project. If they are prepared to make sacrifices and release the A-team players from their other commitments, then clearly they regard the project as having A-grade priority.

The right process

This is where project management manuals focus all their attention. If you have the right problem, sponsor and team, the chances are that you will find the right process. Even when things go awry, you will have enough fire-power in the team to correct your course.

Beyond the elaborate world of Gantt charts and PERT charts, there are three basics to the right process:

1 Start at the end and work backwards.

2 Figure out the minimum number of steps required to get there.

3 Create an effective governance process.

> Starting at the start is never a good idea.

Starting at the start is never a good idea. Define the end outcome as clearly as possible before the start so that everyone knows where they are heading. Knowing the destination minimises the risks of deviations *en route* and cost escalations from contractors.

If you know the end point, then figure out the minimum number of steps required to get there. There are always staffers who can discover bottomless pits of detail to fall into. The challenge for the leader is to make it simple so that everyone stays focused on what is really important. By looking for the minimum number of steps, you will also be defining the critical path (which events need to happen before others can be started), which will also make it much easier to control and monitor progress.

Effective governance is essential. A good way to escalate costs and time is to have vague goals, change your mind frequently and make decisions slowly. This often happens where there is a political environment and not all the constituencies are truly aligned. Clear goals and clear decision-making processes are vital. The other governance trap is to have no governance – many projects are started but have no effective follow-through from top management. You should insist on continued oversight from top management. This helps when it comes to keeping the project on track and overcoming obstacles. It also helps maintain the visibility of the project. A successful project which is invisible to top management does not help its leader much.

Chapter 27

Handling conflicts

There are conflicts in the best-run organisations. The leader should be highly suspicious if there is no conflict, because organisations are set up for conflict.

Let's emphasise this point. In any organisation there is a limited pot of money, management time, skills and resources. Different products, functions and regions will inevitably have different perspectives and priorities. They are all bidding for the same limited resource pot. The ensuing bidding war between departments may be civilised or it may be underhand, political and nasty. In any event, there is a contest and a conflict going on. For many leaders in the middle, the competition is not some abstract organisation in the marketplace. Your real competition is sitting at a desk nearby, competing for the same resources and the same promotion.

> Conflict is not about people or personalities, it is about positions and priorities.

If we recognise that conflict is a natural fact of life in any organisation, we can take the first step towards dealing with it. Conflict is not about people or personalities, it is about positions and priorities.

I asked all our leaders how they dealt with conflict. They all homed in on the same set of principles:

- **Never avoid conflict**. Embrace it. Conflict is how priorities are set and decisions are made. It develops the leadership and interpersonal skills of the emerging leader.
- **Depersonalise the conflict**. Never take conflict personally, even if it is meant that way. Focus on the issues and interests at stake, not the personalities.
- **Detach yourself**. Observe what is happening and do not get emotionally involved. Lose your temper, lose the argument. Think how a leader or role model you admire would handle the situation. One leader called this 'putting on the mask of leadership'. You may have boiling emotions inside, but present the mask of your ideal leader and use that to guide your actions.

Occasionally, some conflicts do become emotional and unpleasant – humans, unlike computers, do have emotions. These events are rare but dangerous. If they are mishandled, even the innocent party becomes tainted by the event. At times like this, a simple model helps as a guide. Try to remember this: FEAR to EAR.

FEAR stands for the natural reaction to outright hostility. It also stands for how we feel before seeing the CEO for the first time. It was a helpful emotion when our ancestors faced a sabre-toothed tiger: it would alert them to fight or flight. Fighting or fleeing at the first sight of the CEO is not helpful.

The wrong response is to let FEAR take over, as follows:

Fight furiously.
Engage enemy emotionally.
Argue against anyone.
Retaliate, refute, repudiate reason.

If it is your last day at work, using FEAR is a good way to go down. However, take the F out of FEAR and you are left with EAR, which is what you should use to start listening. EAR stands for:

Empathise.
Agree the problem.
Resolve the way forward.

The temptation is to go straight to resolving the way forward. This simply invites more argument; the other side will knock down anything you say. You need to calm them down. Empathise with them. This does not mean hugging them, it means using active listening skills, which we will cover later. As you listen, you will find out more about the real nature of their difficulty and why they feel so threatened. Do not try to argue, try to understand. Win a friend, not an argument. Once you have won a friend, you have a chance of winning the argument if there is any substantive disagreement beneath the emotional froth. You cannot begin to find a solution until you have found the problem you both can agree on. Once you have agreed the root cause of the problem together, you have a chance of finding a way forward.

> **Win a friend, not an argument.**

Chapter 28

Handling crises

Some people are lucky, they never encounter a real career or business crisis. However, most people find they do have a crisis at some point in their careers. It can feel very lonely. The only person who can get you out of the crisis is yourself. The middle of the organisation is where many emerging leaders find themselves bailing out to set up their vegan farm in Vermont. This is natural. The first flush of career enthusiasm has disappeared. The long haul to the top still looks long. Then something happens: the final straw is added to the camel's back.

The difference between success and failure sometimes comes down to persistence. Successful leaders work through their crises and find that Nietzsche was right: 'That which does not kill you, makes you stronger.' Others are mucking out the organic waste on their farms.

How to deal with crises

1 **Recognise the problem early**
 Don't go into denial; don't avoid the crisis which will not resolve itself.

2 **Take control**
 Step up to the mark; offer solutions, not problems; have a plan.

3 **Act fast**
 Avoid analysis paralysis; drive to action; focus on outcomes.

4   Focus on what you can do and do it

Build momentum and confidence, even through small initial actions. Don't worry about what you cannot control: you cannot control it.

5   Find plenty of support

Don't be the lone hero; find the people, money, skills and power barons and supporters who can collectively deliver the solution.

6   Over-communicate

Dispel fear, uncertainty, doubt and confusion; be clear and consistent in your messaging. Have a simple story to tell about where you are going and how you will get there.

7   Be positive

You will be remembered as much for how you behaved as for what you did, so be the role model others follow. Set the standard for those around you.

8   Avoid blame

Give praise to those who help; don't look back and analyse problems or point the finger of blame; create a positive, action-focused culture, not a culture of fear and inaction.

9   Show empathy

Recognise the concerns of others; manage your own feelings and fears; wear the mask of leadership and project confidence and empathy.

10   Make the most of crises

Crises are opportunities to make your mark, stand out from your peers and make a difference. The more you encounter crises, the better you become at dealing with them.

The best way to prepare for crises is to develop resilience early on. Having crises and flirting with failure is not easy for a 20-something person. But if the worst comes to the worst, they can start again a little older and much wiser. Doing an MBA is a safe and prestigious way for a 20-something person to start over again.

In contrast, the 40 year old who has never had a crisis has what one CEO called 'brittle' confidence – they look good, sound good and seem confident, but when they face a real challenge or crisis, they crumble. They have no

> The best way to prepare for crises is to develop resilience early on.

reserves to call on. They make a sad sight as they justify why they are happy to be leaving the rat race and how they had always dreamed of organic farming.

Many graduate training programmes do not develop resilience. They test the graduate's appetite for hard work, but that is not the same as resilience. Teach First is an exception. Top graduates spend two years teaching in some of the most challenging schools in the UK. This is, potentially, a brutal experience. But these graduates develop a depth of confidence, resilience and people skills that can never be acquired by their better-paid peers who spend their first two years staring at computer screens trading bonds or doing research. Leaders of the future need to take risks and learn about adversity and resilience early in their careers. Trying to learn these things when you are a 40-something is tough.

The leaders who talked about responding to crises talked about the importance of knowing yourself. Some people let their identity become swamped by their job. When the crisis hits, or when they retire, they have nothing to fall back on. They have become dependent on their job – they live to work. Nearly all the leaders I interviewed had active lives outside work. This gives them a level of independence that makes them better able to deal with challenges.

Ultimately, individuals need to know themselves. Leadership is not for everyone, nor is it necessary for everyone. If you prefer fishing, then focus on that.

Chapter 29

Negotiate your budget and targets

S uccess is often defined by the results you achieve. Logically, this means that you should strive for the best results possible. But there is another way of defining success:

Success = Results minus Expectations

In practice, this is the formula against which you will be judged. This is the world of MBO (management by objectives) and KPIs (key performance indicators). These are grand and formal ways of talking about expectations. This means that you have to work on two items: delivering results and setting expectations. Nearly all of the training and support you receive will be about achieving results. The other half of the equation, setting expectations, is more or less ignored. But it is vital to your ability to be seen to succeed. Naive managers often accept 'challenging' targets because it sounds macho to do so. In contrast, more experienced managers will set expectations low, which then makes it easy to beat the target.

The importance of managing expectations can be seen in the next table. The naive manager accepts a challenging target and delivers results that are better than the more experienced manager. The crucial difference is that the experienced manager negotiates low expectations. At year end, the naive manager finds missed targets lead to a poor review and plenty of remedial support, while the experienced manager enjoys a good bonus for slightly worse results, as shown in the table.

	Naive manager	Experienced manager
Target	150	100
Outcome achieved	125	120
Results minus expectations	−25	+20

You may think this sort of game playing is unworthy of any serious leader, but all leaders do this. Watch what happens when a new CEO takes over. The first thing he (95% of CEOs of top firms are still male) does is to get all the skeletons out of the cupboard. He paints a picture of imminent disaster; there may be a profit warning. Fortunately, he happens to be the hero who can turn things around. He has set expectations low and can then over-deliver, proving that he is the hero he claims to be.

If you are a leader, you will be aware of this game playing; you will have played it yourself. Inevitably, there are two sides to this game. If you are on the receiving end of targets, you want to set expectations low. If you are setting targets, you want to set them high. You will hear all sorts of reasons why your target is unreasonable. There are times when it pays to be unreasonable, and setting targets is one of those times. If you set low targets, you can be sure that you will achieve low results – targets tend to be self-fulfilling prophecies.

> If you set low targets, you can be sure that you will achieve low results – targets tend to be self-fulfilling.

When it comes to budgets, the same principles apply but in reverse. If you are setting budgets, you want to set them low to make scarce resources go as far as possible. If you are receiving a budget, you want as much as possible so that you have the resources to support your goals. The difference can be seen in the next table.

	Leader Setting budgets and targets	Manager Receiving budgets and targets
Budget	Set low budget	Demand high budget
Target	Set high target	Demand low target

Essentially, budgets and targets are a negotiation. Treat them that way. The leader is like the customer, wanting as much as possible for the least expense. The manager is like the provider, wanting as much money (budget) for the least effort. If you accept the orthodoxy of the annual budget cycle, you will find all the cards are stacked against you. By the time your part of the budget is reviewed, expectations will have been set already and you will have minimal opportunity to change those expectations.

So how do you negotiate the right budget and targets? Here are four things you can do:

1   Strike early.

2   Tell a story …

3   Understand the process.

4   Manage this year's performance.

Strike early

Set expectations very early, before the formal budget cycle starts. Early in the cycle there is plenty of room to manoeuvre. As the process evolves, more and more decisions are being made and you will have less and less ability to influence the outcome. You have to be proactive. Instead of waiting for the formal process to reach you, use your informal network to influence the process from the first day.

Tell a story …

… and keep on telling it. You are the expert in your area; it takes time and effort for others to dig into your data and challenge you.

Use this imbalance of knowledge to your advantage. Show that there are particular reasons why your unit next year will face unusual, even unprecedented, challenges which will require a low target and a high budget. Make sure you have assembled all your facts so that you cannot be challenged successfully. Then keep on pushing your story and pushing your facts relentlessly. If you stay quiet, any sort of budget and targets could be inflicted on you.

> Keep on pushing your story and pushing your facts relentlessly.

Understand the process

Know when the budget cycle starts, who is involved and when the broad framework is decided. Make sure you influence the broad framework by making your case to the right people at the right time. The right people may well be two levels above you, in which case you need a simple story for them which you can tell them in a 20-second conversation when you meet them by chance in the corridor. Make sure your chance meeting in the corridor happens and be ready for it. Be ready for a more detailed discussion with key staffers who may be in finance or planning and will be driving the top-down process. Don't wait for the top-down process to work its way down to you – by then it is too late and your fate will have largely been settled.

Manage this year's performance

If you are having a great year, then top management will take this year's results as the baseline for next year. If you worked minor miracles this year, next year you will have to work major miracles. When you realise this year is going to be outstanding, you might want to start massaging your numbers – bring expenses forward, delay recognising revenues. Create a baseline that is acceptable for next year.

Chapter 30

Control your costs

A quick way to fail as a leader is to fail to control your costs. Missing budget unexpectedly, even by a small amount, is a disaster because it:

- shows you are not in control: you are no longer seen to be reliable
- surprises your bosses, who dislike surprises
- causes problems across the organisation, which will have to make up for your shortfall.

You cannot become an outstanding leader through cost control alone. But you cannot become a leader at all if you do not control costs well. Here are ten tips for avoiding budget disaster.

Manage your budget

1 Frontload performance
   Use the 52/48 rule. Target to achieve 52% of your results with 48% of your budget in the first half of the year. Then target to deliver 52/48 of the first six months' budget in the first three months. Surprises later in the year are rarely good – the 52/48 rule gives you protection against unpleasant surprises. It is also an effective way of pushing your team to better performance.

2   Review your position frequently

Review your position at least once a month. If any of your units are behind schedule, you need to help them and push them early. Frequent reviews also send a message to your team that budget discipline is a high priority for you and for them.

3   Act early

If your budget is going the wrong way, act early. The later you leave it, the worse things become. You will not look like you are in control and you will have less time to make up the shortfall.

4   Use finance and use controls

Fraud and financial cock-ups are what happen to other people … until they happen to you. Financial controls are painful, but they are there for a good reason. Make friends with finance and internal audit, and make sure that their controls are being followed properly.

5   Watch accruals

These can wreck a budget. If you commit to an expense later in the year, recognise it now so that you are not surprised when the expense hits you later on. Accruals have a habit of being invisible until too late.

6   Spend smartly

You know that at year end you will be squeezed to make up for shortfalls elsewhere. Your budget is likely to be cut. Discretionary spend gets cut first. If you have important discretionary items, such as a team offsite meeting, do not leave it until the fourth quarter.

7   Squeeze hard

Your team will always have reasons why they need to spend more. Set a basic rule: you can spend more if you find the savings elsewhere. If you see opportunities to save money, such as delaying a budgeted hire for a couple of months, then take it where possible.

8   Sandbag

Build reserves. If you are seen to be ahead of budget, then your goals will simply be raised mid-year. Your savings will be used to offset shortfalls elsewhere. Avoid declaring success too early, if you can, because you will be punished for it.

9 Work the numbers

There is always discretion about how costs and revenues are recognised and whether spending is capital or current. Use this flexibility to your advantage: when you are falling short at year end, this discretion can just tip the balance in your favour. If you are way ahead of budget, you can use this discretion to reduce your year-end outcome – this allows a fast start to next year off a lower baseline.

10 Set an example

Show that you care about the budget. Don't spend lavishly yourself. And focus on the right things – don't try to control access to the photocopier, control the numbers that can make a difference to your year-end outcome.

Why financial control matters

We started up a new charity with big ambitions and few resources. So we threw everything we had into providing our core service. Things like finance were just a drain on our precious resources, an unproductive and costly overhead.

We started to change our mind the month when we suddenly found out we were about to miss payroll. Our finance manager had not spotted that until too late. So we decided it was time to find a new finance manager and spend a bit more to recruit the right person.

The next finance manager was more competent, but not quite competent enough to get away with writing unauthorised cheques to himself. Luckily, the bank spotted that one for us and we escaped.

So now we decided to invest properly in finance. Our new finance director seemed competent and, unusually for a finance director, was popular with the staff. This might have been something to do with her sideline in selling cheap music CDs to them. When I visited her, I found she kept large amounts of money in shoeboxes beneath her sofa. I asked her about this: 'That is my CD money,' she said, 'and I really don't trust banks. Better to keep it where I can see it.'

A few weeks later she did not turn up for work, which was unprecedented. Her absence became clear when we saw her on the news: she had been helping an armed gang rob a bank. No wonder she did not trust banks.

So we finally recognised that we had to beef up finance to make it bulletproof. Which was just as well: a few years later it helped us spot a newish member of the finance team trying on a false supplier invoice fraud.

Fraud and financial malpractice only happen to other people, don't they?

Chapter 31

Making decisions in uncertainty

M ost decisions are relatively easy. But not all. Occasionally you are faced with a high-stakes decision which is shrouded in fog and ambiguity. This fog appears for various reasons:

- Uncertainty: not all the facts may be apparent and the criteria for making a decision may not be known or may be contested.

- High stakes: the consequences of making the wrong decision could be severe, not just for the firm but also for yourself.

- Politics: the consequences of a decision may be uneven across your organisation, so different groups will start fighting hard for their preferred option.

- Multiple perspectives: the opportunity will look very different depending on what angle you look at it from and what criteria you use to evaluate each option.

- Complexity: this comes from having too many conflicting and overlapping options. When faced with too much choice, paralysis and inaction are normal outcomes.

Faced with this sort of fog, what do you do? One senior executive has a simple approach: he tosses a coin. His reasoning is that if a decision is finely balanced between two options, then both options are about as good as each other. You may as well toss a coin and drive to action. The world is rarely that simple. You normally face a wide range of options with quite different impacts, risk profiles and cost–benefits. You are not going to be comparing apples with apples, you will be comparing apples and bicycles. They are hard to compare.

Here are the techniques effective leaders often use.

Trust your judgement

You are the expert in your area and if you are not the expert, you should not be there. In coaching executives I find many worry about making a decision. Close questioning often reveals that they know what the decision should be, but they are unsure whether they can gain enough support for the way forward, or whether they can neutralise some tough opposition. Think carefully whether the decision is genuinely tough, or whether the politics of the decision are tough.

> Think carefully whether the decision is genuinely tough, or whether the politics of the decision are tough.

Seek advice

This helps in three ways:

1   The simple act of talking an issue through often crystallises that issue and you will discover the way forward for yourself.

2   By looking at the problem from another perspective, you will often find a completely different solution, or a much better way of framing an existing solution.

3   As you seek advice, you build support for the way forward. When colleagues have been involved in making a decision, they are more likely to support than if you just present them with your solution.

Take responsibility

If you go too far in seeking advice, you land up losing control over the decision. You cannot abdicate responsibility for making key decisions, unless you are prepared to look weak and lose power and credibility. Seeking advice is fine – the advice will help you frame your decision – but do not let anyone else make the decision for you.

Understand the problem

All students are taught to answer the question in an exam. At least they know what the exam question is. In leadership, the question is often never stated, you have to work out what the question is. A good way to start is to ask: 'Who wants to address this problem/ opportunity and why?' Once you know the who, what and why about the problem or opportunity, the solution often presents itself clearly. You know you have the right problem only when you know what the criteria are for evaluating each option and there is no argument about those criteria.

Size the prize

This is the opposite side of the coin from understanding the problem. Know what the desired outcome is. Evaluate each option in terms of that prize. As we have seen earlier, if you can convert the prize into a financial number, that often helps create a sense of urgency and commitment from everyone who is involved in the decision. Only after you know the potential benefits of each solution is it worth exploring the risks and issues of each solution. If you start by looking at the risks and issues you will not just depress yourself, you will also convince yourself that there is no viable option at all.

Avoid perfection

A good way of making sure that a decision is never made is to seek the perfect solution. We live in a messy world where perfection rarely exists. It is better to seek the practical over the perfect. If you were playing golf, you would not get far if you only ever wanted to hit a hole in one. It is better to work towards your goal in steps rather than hope for the perfect shot. Closely linked to this is the need to avoid too much analysis. Analysis is often a smoke screen, which is used to avoid having to make a decision. Calling in the consultants is a good way of delaying a decision, deflecting the blame and abdicating responsibility – it is not the act of a leader.

> We live in a messy world where perfection rarely exists.

Beyond these informal techniques, there are myriad formal decision-making tools and techniques. These range from Bayesian analysis (which can be used for major investment decisions) through to brainstorming in groups. In between there are endless tools to help you frame the decision: fishbone analysis, Pareto analysis, decision trees, SWOT analysis, cost–benefit analysis, conjoint analysis, force-field analysis and many more. Each technique has its high priests, who are consultants: they jealously protect the virtue, value and integrity of their particular approach versus all others. The good news is that they all provide ways of helping you structure your thinking; done well they may also help bring together decision makers to create a new insight or to produce a consensus. Done badly, you become slaves to someone else's process. Use these tools if they help you, but do not use them to avoid making the decision.

Chapter 32

Influencing decisions

As a leader you cannot make every decision yourself. Some decisions will be beyond your control. That should not stop you influencing decisions that are important to you. Fortunately, there is good evidence on how you can influence decisions, based largely on the work of Nobel Prize winning economist Daniel Kahneman. Despite his academic pedigree, there is plenty of help for the practising leader in his work.

> As a leader, some decisions will be beyond your control.

Here is how you can influence decisions in your favour.

How to influence decisions

1   Anchor the debate on your terms

   Strike early; set the terms of the debate around your agenda. For example, is the moon more or less than 1 million miles from earth? I have no idea, but I have just anchored the debate around 1 million (not 5 million or 100,000).

2   Build your coalition

   Manage disagreements in private. Once they disagree in public, they will be committed to that position and will not change. Meet key people early and in private. Let them change their view without loss of face; publicise any agreements widely to build a bandwagon of support. Find powerful sponsors to endorse your position.

3   Build incremental agreement

Don't scare people by asking for everything at once. Ask individuals to back the one part of your idea where they have relevant expertise (finance, health and safety, etc.).

4   Size the prize

Build a clear, logical case which shows the benefits of your proposed course of action. Quantify the benefits and have them endorsed appropriately.

5   Frame the decision favourably

Align your agenda with the corporate agenda. Frame your idea in the right language and style for each person. Be relentlessly positive.

6   Restrict choice

Don't give too many options that will tend to confuse. If you offer 30 choices, you create confusion and decision paralysis will follow. Offer two or three choices at most. This is normally option A: ideal, expensive and impractical; option B: cheap, nasty and unacceptable; option C: which you want them to pick. Let them lecture you on how awful options A and B are, then look suitably impressed by their insight and advice when they tell you to go with option C.

7   Work risk and loss aversion to your favour

Show that alternatives to your idea are even riskier. Normally the default option is 'do nothing': low cost, low risk and low effort. You have to show that doing nothing is not acceptable.

8   Put idleness to work

Make it easy for people to agree; remove any logistical or administrative hurdles for them.

9   Be persistent

Repetition works. What works? Repetition. Repetition works. Repetition works. Repetition works. Repetition works. Repetition works.

Repetition works. Repetition works. Repetition works. Repetition works. Repetition works. Repetition works. Repetition works. Repetition works. Repetition works. Repetition works. All great advertisers and dictators know that the more you repeat something, the more people believe it. Be persistent and never give up.

10   **Adjust to each individual**

See the world through their eyes. Respect their needs in terms of substance, style and format. Build common cause; align your agendas.

Chapter 33

Use time well

Time is our most valuable resource. We can only spend it once, so we should spend it well. At work, this means you have to think strategically and tactically about how to use your time well.

Time strategies

You can use time well by focusing on three questions:

1 What do I want to achieve?
2 How can I get others to help me?
3 What is my role?

These questions, as we shall see, should look familiar.

What do I want to achieve?

This is the return of your idea. Know what you want to achieve and stay focused on that. You will still have to deal with the day-to-day noise of where you work, but do not let yourself be drowned by the noise.

Using time well?

In the nineteenth century an amateur scientist managed to hitch a lift on a Royal Navy vessel that was going around the world. He spent a large amount of time ashore visiting friends of friends and pursuing his scientific interests. After a few years, he returned to England and

▶

continued to potter away. He did not appear very productive: he never had the chance to master the art of following a meeting, checking email, texting and keeping up with the news all at the same time. Many years later he was encouraged to publish the results of his studies from his trip and beyond. The result, *The Origin of Species*, changed science and changed the way we look at ourselves for ever. Charles Darwin's trip on 'HMS Beagle' was one of the most productive scientific trips ever.

Darwin failed to live up to the current vogue for the hyperactive multi-tasking executive. But he achieved much more because he was much more focused on what he wanted to achieve.

Never confuse activity with achievement.

How can I get others to help me?

The amount of working time available to you is constrained only by budgets and the number of people who work with you. The lone hero who tries to prove themselves and do it all alone will soon burn out, stress out and drop out. Find help, find support and you turn time to your advantage.

What is my role?

As we have seen, when you have a great team that does everything for you, that leaves you with a problem: what is your role and where do you add any value? Answer this and you will find you are highly productive. Normally, the things you have to do and cannot delegate include setting direction; picking, coaching and supporting your team; providing political cover when required and negotiating the right budgets and resourcing for your team.

> Focus on the right goal, with the right team and with the right role.

Time strategy can be summed up as focus on the right goal, with the right team and with the right role for yourself. If you do all of this, you have a chance of being highly productive without being highly stressed.

Time tactics

The goal here is not to attempt to do 12 hours' work in 8 hours, the goal is to achieve 8 hours of progress in 8 hours. If you can do this, you will be well ahead of most of your peers. There is a huge amount of lost time in the average working day, especially in office work where productivity is hard to measure and it is easy to hide.

Useful time tips

1 Set clear goals
   Know what you want to do this month, this week and today. Review your goals regularly and make sure you stay on track. Set your priorities accordingly.

2 Keep a to-do list
   Convert your goals into actions for today. Then check and review at the end of the day. Make sure you are doing the high-priority and tough items, not just the easy and less important tasks.

3 Make it simple
   Big tasks often look daunting, so it is natural to try to avoid them. But even the biggest task can be broken down into small, simple steps. Do this, then start tackling each simple step.

4 Use short-interval scheduling
   Focus on what you can do in 30 minutes or an hour. Perhaps it is no more than making some important phone calls. Once you have done them, tick them off your to-do list and reward yourself with a tea or coffee.

5 Rest
   No one can work well non-stop. You need short breaks, which will help your energy levels and concentration. Resting for 5 minutes an hour can help you have 55 productive minutes in an hour, instead of 60 unproductive minutes.

6 **Have your crisis early**

Living life close to every deadline may be exciting and look dynamic, but it wastes time: you are firefighting, rather than progressing. Finish tasks well ahead of deadlines and you will stay in control and still be able to deal with any unexpected last-minute panics.

7 **Do it once, do it right**

Rework is a major source of wasted time and energy. Aim to touch each piece of paper and each email just once – deal with it and move on. Take the 3D approach to every email: deal with it, delete it or delegate it.

8 **Control your time**

Time thieves are everywhere, stealing your time with unimportant meetings at awkward times. Make sure you attend relevant meetings at convenient times and avoid the rest.

9 **Manage your environment**

If you live in chaos, your time will evaporate amid missing files and distractions on your desk.

10 **Question and challenge**

Review how you spend your time. Keep a time log to see what you really do, how much time is spent reacting to noise, is wasted or is proactively pushing your agenda. Adapt your habits accordingly.

There are three ingenious ways of losing time: procrastination, distractions and multi-tasking.

Procrastination

This is where you avoid important or tough tasks by doing easy, unimportant or irrelevant things. You maintain the illusion of activity without making any real progress. Your to-do list should keep you honest about this and breaking down the difficult tasks into simple steps helps further.

Distractions

Office technology can make us much more productive if we use it well. It can also kill our productivity when we use it poorly. Social media, news feeds and buying and selling stuff are obvious distractions. Perhaps more invidious are office produc-

> Office technology can make us much more productive if we use it well.

tivity tools that invite us to do work we should not do. As a senior leader, leave PowerPoint to people who are better and quicker at it, and cost less – if you want to spend hours that way, do it in your personal time or get a job as a PowerPoint expert.

Multi-tasking

Multi-tasking does not work. For evidence, go into the street and watch someone trying to text and walk at the same time: they do both poorly. Just hope you do not encounter someone trying to drive and text at the same time. You can manage ten tasks over the course of the day, but you cannot do them all at the same time. You have to deal with them one at a time, switching between them during the day as necessary. You can multi-task in sequence, not in parallel.

Chapter 34

Present to persuade

T he Bambara are the largest farming tribe in Mali. They are largely illiterate. But they regard words as being close to gods. They say: 'Words create whole new worlds in the mind; words make people do things; words separate humans from beasts.' Words are powerful. The Bambara say that words should be forged like a blacksmith, woven like a weaver and polished like a cobbler. Not surprisingly, they value restraint in how people talk – better to talk little and well than to talk for the sake of it.

Words can have as much power in the management tribe as they can in the Bambara tribe. We cover the art of communicating, motivating, influencing and coaching one to one in other chapters. Here we will look at the specific challenge of talking to large groups. For emerging leaders these showpiece events can have a disproportionate influence on how they are perceived. Some people are terrified of such events and struggle to shine. The people who think that they are born demagogues often make even worse presentations. Everyone can benefit from learning the basic techniques of presenting effectively.

Effective speaking

It is a truism that an audience is more likely to remember you than your message; in many ways, you are the message. So if you are the king of the mumblers, dress like a tramp and slouch like Quasimodo with a hangover, the chances are that the brilliance of your message will be lost on the audience. In contrast, if you can remember the three Es of communication, even a dull message is likely to come across well:

> An audience is more likely to remember you than your message.

- Energy.
- Enthusiasm.
- Excitement.

It is as hard to fake these three Es as it is to rehearse spontaneity. But there are some things that can help. Some of the 'dos' include:

- **Throw away the script**. With it, you will sound wooden or, worse, like a politician. Instead, memorise your opening so that you can make a good start. Memorise your conclusion so that you can make a good finish. Memorise some choice phrases that you want to insert on your way through – each phrase is a way marker on your speech. You will keep your structure and discipline while sounding spontaneous.

- **Avoid complicated slide presentations**. If you have slides, the principle is to have dumb slides but a smart presenter. The slide might have three or four key words to help the audience anchor where you are – you provide the commentary. The nightmare is to have smart slides which explain everything and a dumb presenter who reads the slides more slowly than the audience does.

- **Stand on the front of your feet**, so that a slip of paper could pass under your heel. Weight on the back of the foot encourages slouching and lowers your energy.

- **Try to stand before going on stage**. If you are sitting down before speaking, all your energy is down. You are likely to over-compensate with a sudden rush of adrenalin.

- **Engage the audience**. Look individuals in the eye, rather than gazing into the middle distance. Billy Graham, the great American preacher, did this with devastating effect. Even in an audience of a thousand, he would pick out individuals and catch their eye for a moment or two, so that they felt they were being addressed personally. No one dared doze off.

- **Vary your pace and pitch**. Dare to slow down when you come to an important point. Give your key points the space to be heard.

- **Keep it simple**. Focus on one or two messages at most. If you have a large audience, focus on the one or two key executives you want to influence. This will let you focus your message, get rid of excess material and tell a simple story.

The three Es are greatly enhanced by two more Es: expertise and enjoyment. If you are expert at your subject, you are more likely to relax and enjoy what you are saying. If you are enjoying it, your audience is likely to enjoy it as well. If you hate it, do not expect the audience to enjoy it. As an experiment, try telling someone about how the cost-allocation system in your organisation works. See whether you fall asleep before they do. Now try recounting one of the most memorable events in your personal or professional life. You will naturally display all five Es: energy, enthusiasm, excitement, expertise and enjoyment. Such a simple exercise shows that we can all speak well – we simply have to transfer our skills onto the big stage.

Making presentations

1 Show energy, enthusiasm and excitement

   If you are not enthusiastic about your topic, no one else will be. Enjoy your talk and there is a chance that others will also enjoy it.

2 Target your talk

Be clear who you are talking to, what it is they need to hear and why they need to hear it. This will let you reduce and simplify your message. In a large group, focus your message on the one or two people you most want to influence.

3 Tell a story

Show 'this is where we are, this is where we will get to and this is how we will get there'. Make the story clear from the start of your talk. Stick to one simple theme that everyone can remember.

4 Engage your audience

At minimum, focus on each individual one at a time and use eye contact; even better, make it interactive, ask and answer questions, and create small group work.

5 Keep it short

Your presentation is not complete when you can say no more; it is complete when you can say no less. Focus on your core message for your target audience.

6 Ditch PowerPoint

If you must use it, then have a smart presenter and dumb slides, simple slides with few words that you bring to life. Avoid smart slides with lots of data that a dumb presenter then reads slowly.

7 Seek help in preparation

Find a coach who can tell you who the audience will be and what they want. Get an editor to review your slides. If necessary, get coaching on presenting skills and get help with your script.

8 Practise, practise, practise

The more often you present, the better you get. Do the same presentation many times and you build confidence and expertise; you can relax and enjoy.

9 Arrive early

Make sure all the logistics work and the room layout is right. Have a back-up computer or memory stick. Do a final check with the organisers that you have the right expectations. Understand what has happened before your talk and be ready to adjust your talk if required.

10   **Start well and end well**

Script your opening so that you start well, however nervous you may feel. Script your finish to end on a high (not 'any questions?') and script some choice phrases in between which can mark the start and end of each section of your talk.

Chapter 35

Making meetings work

Meetings are a wonderful substitute for work or responsibility. They are also the essence of management – they consume time and can have high impact. So it pays to have effective meetings, to minimise wasted time and maximise impact. Now think of what proportion of the meetings you have to attend is truly effective. You may be lucky, in which case move on to the next section. You may be like the majority of managers who find too much of a limited day being drained away in ineffective meetings.

> Meetings, like liquorice allsorts, come in all shapes and sizes.

Meetings, like liquorice allsorts, come in all shapes and sizes. They range from informal one-to-one meetings to major conferences, from formal decision-making meetings of the board to brainstorming meetings of the staff. For the sake of brevity and sanity, this is not the time or place to explore every flavour of meeting.

Effective meetings come down to three principles:

1　Right **purpose**.
2　Right **people**.
3　Right **process**.

Forests have been destroyed describing effective meeting processes. Let us save some trees and concentrate on the right people and the right purpose. If you have these, you are 80% of the way to success. If you do not have them, you are 100% of the way to failure.

The right people and the right purpose

After one particularly mind-numbing all-day meeting, Dean, one of my mentors, looked very happy. I asked him what was wrong with him. He should have looked as unhappy as I felt. He explained he had three rules for any meeting. He applied them whether he was leading or attending the meeting, and it always helped him get a good result. Since then, the rules have been a productive guide for me to ensure that meetings have the right purpose and the right people. The three rules for any meeting are:

1   What do I want to learn?

2   What will I contribute?

3   What happens next?

Let's look at Dean's rules as applied to attending a meeting and leading a meeting.

Attending a meeting

Dean went to the all-day meeting with a clear agenda, which had little to do with the official agenda. There were three people he had wanted to talk to, but they had all been elusive. He wanted to get some information and ideas from them. That was his learning rule. He also realised that the meeting gave him the chance to influence the CEO on one agenda item. He bided his time, then moved in decisively on the one issue that mattered. Because he talked sparingly, when he did speak he commanded attention. He had fulfilled his contribution rule. By having both a clear learning and contribution objective, he had a series of follow-up actions with the CEO and the three people he had met. Everyone else had left the meeting frustrated because nothing had been achieved in the formal agenda. Dean left happy because he had gone to the meeting with a clear intent and purpose, which he had achieved.

Leading a meeting

Dean applied his three meeting rules to meetings he chaired. He used the rules to decide who should attend. He expected each person to contribute something *and* to do something by way of follow-up *and* to learn something useful. People could contribute by having decision-making power, having expertise or having resources they could contribute.

Resist the temptation to seek safety in numbers. More people reduce effectiveness. Senior people want bag carriers to be present because they have the detail; bag carriers want to be there to get exposure to the senior managers. If the senior people cannot master the detail, they should not be there. They probably should not be senior managers.

> Resist the temptation to seek safety in numbers.

You can see the safety-in-numbers mentality even in the executive suite. Normally the discussion dissolves into a series of bilateral discussions between the CEO and individual directors. Each director is a fully signed-up member of the mutual preservation society. The only rule of membership is 'I will not trample on your turf if you do not trample on mine'. So group discussion does not exist. Instead, each director plays a game of intellectual ping-pong with the CEO while the other directors are spectators waiting for their turn to have a game with the CEO.

Dean refused to let this happen. He would apply his three rules not just to the meeting as a whole but to each agenda item individually. If an item was best handled bilaterally, he would not bring it to the larger group. This made his meetings small and effective.

Also, everyone knew that the meetings were going to be effective and relevant to them, so they made a point of attending.

The right process

Having the right people and the right purpose for a meeting is essential. It also helps to have the right process.

Effective meetings follow the same rules as the radio parlour game 'Just a Minute'. The object of the game is to speak for one minute on a chosen subject without hesitation, deviation or repetition. It is very difficult. The same principles should apply to the meeting process – to manage it without hesitation, deviation or repetition.

Hesitation is a product of starting late. It is nearly mandatory for senior people to turn up last or late. This shows that:

- they are very busy
- their time is more important than yours, so you can wait.

They may be answering emails or practising the banjo, but they will still want you to wait. It is a common discourtesy that customers visit on suppliers, professionals on their clients, call-centre staff on their callers and managers on their staff. Live with it. Otherwise, putting up a clock in the office at least helps induce some guilt in those who are not shameless. As a leader, you can set an example: be prompt and show that time is valuable and individuals are respected.

> Be prompt and show that time is valuable and individuals are respected.

Hesitation also comes from a loose timetable. Time the meeting to be as short as possible to force the pace. Sitting down is not mandatory. The Privy Council meets standing up. This is a good way of keeping long-winded politicians short. It was particularly short when the late Queen Mother, aged 98, presided over the meeting.

There are times when you should never hesitate. Never be disturbed by interruptions. Leaders should remain totally focused. I learned this in Manila during a period with many electricity outages. The first time it happened, the room went pitch black. I hesitated: big error. Next time it happened, I carried on my presentation as if nothing had happened. The discussion flowed on in pitch blackness.

Deviation is a common cause of delay. People ramble off the subject or delve into minutiae. A good chairperson should not let this happen. If you set up the 'Just a Minute' rules at the start of the meeting, it becomes easy to challenge deviators; you can even keep score during the meeting. At a minimum, make people give the headline before the text, as in a newspaper column. The headline tells people whether it is worth listening to or reading. It forces the speaker to think about what they want to say before they launch into a ramble.

Repetition normally happens when someone thinks they are not being heard properly. So they keep coming back to the same point time and again, and again, and again. The rolling of eyeballs and looks of disbelief from everyone reinforce the repeater's belief that they are not being understood. Do not roll your eyeballs at repetition. Paraphrase the speaker to check you have heard what they are saying – this shows them that you are listening and they may shut up. If they raise the same point, repeat the paraphrase. Even the most obtuse participant should figure out that they have been heard and they are being repetitive.

The right process is helped by the right context. Dark, stuffy rooms do not help. The seating layout in the room does not have to be taken as given. I have become an expert furniture mover over many years of arranging meetings. How people sit affects the dynamics of the meeting. Having tea and coffee available is great, but the smell of hot food arriving at the back of the room loses an audience fast. Figure out the logistics that will make the meeting work for you and the attendees.

Chapter 36

Listen to influence

Good listening is devastatingly effective. Like sincerity and spontaneity, it is difficult to fake. Good sales people and good leaders, like most normal people, have one mouth and two ears and they use them in that proportion. People like listening to the one person they truly trust and admire: themselves. Give people the chance and they will talk themselves into submission.

> Good leaders, like most normal people, have one mouth and two ears and they use them in that proportion.

Each of the following three cases includes two approaches. Think about which approach is likely to be more effective in each case.

- **The sales call**. Spend 15 minutes telling your client about the wonders of new miracle Sudso, which cleans up the competition, and then ask for the sale. Naturally, the client will find a thousand objections and, at best, negotiate like crazy on price. Or let the client talk about their competitive situation and direct your questions to helping them focus on the sorts of challenges that miracle Sudso happens to address. They will discover that they need Sudso and you can be their partner in solving their problem. You have moved from being a sales person to a partner.

- **The staff challenge.** Your staff bring you a problem. You are the heroic leader who is the fountain of all knowledge, so you solve their problem and tell them exactly what to do. They leave the room feeling that you are clever, but they have no ownership over the solution. And they have learned dependence: it is easier to bring problems to you than it is to solve them themselves. Or you ask questions, let them figure out the answer and let them own both the problem and the solution, to which they are now committed because they feel it is their idea.

- **The performance review.** Tell the staff member that they are underperforming. Be clear about what has gone wrong and what remedial action is expected. Watch them retreat, depressed or angry or in denial. Alternatively, let them talk through their performance. Ask questions to make them focus on what they can do better and how they can do better. Watch them leave, feeling cautiously optimistic that they have a way forward. They will also feel grateful and loyal to a boss who has listened and cared.

Listening is much more difficult than talking. Active listening requires acute thinking and acute questioning. There are three fairly straightforward things you can do to develop listening skills, apart from putting tape across your mouth to make you shut up:

1 Paraphrase.

2 Ask open questions.

3 Debrief.

Paraphrase

This is very simple and forces you to listen. When someone has said something and has reached a natural pause, it is tempting to pitch in with your own point of view. Avoid temptation. Instead, summarise in your own words what you heard the other person say. This does not signify agreement – it signifies only that you understood what they said and that you were listening. If you summarise incorrectly, they will correct you quickly and you will have avoided misunderstanding. If you summarise correctly, they will think you are pretty smart because you have understood them. They will then feel emboldened to embellish what they have said. Paraphrasing builds understanding and respect. As a simple test, try paraphrasing what this section has said. As you paraphrase, you should also find it much easier to remember what has been said. If you say it, you remember it.

Ask open questions

This is a real art form, which we have visited before. It is worth a brief recap. The right open questions will get the other person to focus and reflect on the right issues the right way. The key part of open questioning is to encourage the other person to give rich answers. The one thing to avoid is a closed question, which results in a yes/no type answer.

Closed questions invite someone to take a position, which they then feel the need to defend. Avoid boxing them into a corner. Questions that fall into this trap often begin:

- 'Do you agree ...?'
- 'Shall we go to ...?'
- 'How much is ...?'

If you know you will get the 'right' answer to these questions at the end of a discussion, they may be acceptable. If you get the 'wrong' answer, you will find yourself taking opposing positions and you are in a win/lose discussion.

Open questions invite rich answers. They avoid boxing people into a corner too early and allow options to be explored. As you let people talk, you let their trust in you build. Open questions often begin:

- 'Why did they …?'
- 'What happened when …?'
- 'How would you …?'

> Letting people talk takes more time than simply telling them what to do.

Inevitably, letting people talk takes more time than simply telling them what to do. The lazy and heroic form of leadership is to tell everyone what to do. The longer and less heroic route is more productive. It teaches people to think for themselves, to own their own problems and to find their own solutions.

Debrief

If there were more than two of you at the meeting, always try to debrief around three questions:

1 What did you hear/observe during the meeting?

2 How were they reacting?

3 Who does what next?

This need only take a few minutes. Inevitably, you will find that two people saw and heard different things. You will get far more value and intelligence out of the meeting by a quick debrief than by trying to take notes in the meeting. Note-taking simply gets in the way; it prevents observation. Writing obstructs thinking about how to manage the conversation. It puts the other people on their guard.

Chapter 37
Write effectively

G ood business writing is one of those oxymorons that is up there with military intelligence, social services and head office help.* It is definitely a case of 'Do as I say, not do as I do.' None of us is likely to write as well as our favourite novelist or screen writer. But at least we can save our colleagues from the kind of drivel that they impose on us from time to time.

For many years I was beaten up by an editor who kept on pulling my work apart. Eventually, I figured he caught me consistently on just five rules which I always broke, and still do too often:

1 Write for the reader.
2 Tell a story.
3 Keep it simple and short.
4 Make it positive in substance and in style.
5 Support assertions with facts.

This sounds easy. It is not – it requires real discipline and focus.

1 Write for the reader

Faced with the daily deluge of email, you may occasionally wonder why you are wasting your time on so much trivia. Much of it was

---

*Try also: civil servant, controlled chaos, easy payments, collective responsibility, committee decision, job security, gourmet pizza, non-alcoholic beer, objective opinions and quick fixes.

not meant for you; you have been copied in on stuff on a just-in-case basis. But some emails have clearly been written for you personally. Even if they are poorly typed, with spelling errors and bad grammar, you are likely to read them; they are relevant to your needs and interests. The good writer thinks themselves into the position of the reader and writes for that person. When this happens, clarity and focus are achieved. You can drop much of what you could write and focus on what the other person needs to read. Avoid the trap of writing for yourself.

2 Tell a story

This does not have to be a literal story, like a nursery story or an adventure tale. Telling a story in business terms means marshalling the facts so that a coherent theme comes out, with a beginning (here's the problem or opportunity), a middle (here's the detail) and an end (so what do we do next?). The story should pass the elevator test: you can summarise it to your boss in a fast-moving elevator going a short distance. The virtue of telling a story is that it helps cut out all the noise that will confuse the message.

> The virtue of telling a story is that it helps cut out all the noise that will confuse the message.

Think of all the communications you receive every day – you really remember the headlines, not the detail. Focus first on getting the headline right, then marshal the minimum required to back up the headline.

3 Keep it simple and short

Churchill wrote a long letter to his wife, Clementine, during the war. At the end he added a postscript: 'I am sorry I wrote you such a long letter: I did not have time to write you a short one.' Writing short is much harder than writing long. It requires real mental discipline.

P&G used to be home of the one-page memo: young brand assistants had to summarise the entire progress of their brand for two months in one page. It may have been single spaced with no margins, but everyone kept to the same discipline, which forces the writer to focus on what is important and does not confuse the reader with irrelevant detail.

Documents, like diamonds, benefit from good cutting.

Another thing that helps the reader is to keep words and sentences short. Jargon, fancy words and complicated sentences impress the writer more than the reader. Documents, like diamonds, benefit from good cutting. Your document is not complete when you can write no more, it is complete when you can write no less.

4 Make it positive in substance and in style

People prefer to hear about opportunities and solutions rather than problems and difficulties. Be positive and sound positive. The classic bureaucratic trap is to write passively and in the third person: 'It has been ascertained that the following 27 points were deemed … to make your eyes glaze over with tedium.'

5 Support assertions with facts

The alert reader's nonsense detector will start squawking loudly when it encounters vague power words such as:

- important (to who and why?)
- strategic (important with bells on)
- urgent (not to me it isn't).

Avoid vague power words unless you can back them up. If it is important, show why. Supporting assertions with facts can also include using illustrations, examples and references to support your case. An unsupported assertion is always open to challenge.

Chapter 38

Read for insight

W e have a problem. You are reading this. So why on earth do you need to learn how to read when you are already reading?

There is a difference between reading for pleasure and reading for business. I hope you get some pleasure from reading this, even if you are not a masochist. But I will assume that you are really reading this for business. You have my commiserations. By way of apology, let me tell you a story.

Reading with prejudice

We were all sitting together in the old-fashioned partners' office. We all knew what all the other partners were doing; we did not need email because we had ears. Most of the partners had lightning-quick minds. The exception was Bob, whose mind moved at the pace of a three-legged mule. And yet the staff loved him and thought that he was brighter than the rest of us. This was deeply irritating to us.

One day I noticed Bob making some notes and I asked him what he was doing. 'I have some associates coming in. They are going to show me a draft of a document. I have not seen it yet. This is their little test to see if I am any use at giving feedback and to see if I am smart enough to understand their brilliant draft.'

I thought about this. I had always thought that associates bringing drafts was our chance to test them. Then I realised that Bob was right: they are

▶

also testing our ability as partners to add value to them. I asked Bob why he was making notes if he had not seen the draft in advance.

'Easy,' said Bob. 'I always make a note of three things before seeing a document blind or listening to a presentation. First, I note my own view of the subject. I do not want to be swayed by their internal logic. The better their logic is, the more difficult it is to challenge unless you already have a clear point of view yourself. I do not read openly; I read with prejudice. It makes me a better critic.'

'Ouch,' I thought. I always read openly, and I always found it difficult to rise above the brilliance of the internal logic presented to me. I asked him what else he was noting.

'Second, I note down all the topics I expect to see covered. This helps me spot those things that are hardest to spot – things that aren't there. It always surprises them when I see the invisible gaps.'

'And last?' I asked.

'I make a quick note of any coaching points I want to cover with them,' replied Bob. 'It may be about writing style, analytic techniques, data presentation, whatever. They like it when I can give them something practical and positive to go away and work on.'

I suddenly realised that I had never learned how to read. I had read like an empty vessel waiting to be filled with other people's stuff. Socially, this is an enjoyable way of reading a novel. In managerial terms, it pays to read with prejudice and with an agenda:

- Know your point of view.
- Know what you expect to be covered.
- Have some coaching points ready.

Naturally, it is impossible to do this exercise for every email you receive, and you probably do not want to spoil reading for pleasure with this discipline. But if the meeting, presentation or document is important, it pays to go in properly prepared. Of course, you might discover other things as you review the document or listen to the presentation, but at least you are now reading or listening with focused intent.

> It is better to read a little well than a lot poorly.

Naturally, those of you who already read with intent are probably wondering why this reading section is missing one critical element: the art of speed reading. This is because my prejudice is that it is better to read a little well than a lot poorly.

Chapter 39

Work the numbers

M anagers use statistics the same way drunks use lampposts – for support, not illumination. Numbers are armies of facts that can be marshalled in support of a business case. Numbers are rarely objective; they can all be spun and manipulated. Politicians know this better than anyone.

> Managers use statistics the same way drunks use lampposts – for support, not illumination.

The numbers game finds its apotheosis in the spreadsheet. In the days before spreadsheets, senior managers could terrorise junior managers by checking their calculations. The senior manager would quickly add up a few columns or rows and if the number did not come to 100, the inquisition would start. Spreadsheets have destroyed this form of terror. Numeracy is no longer necessary to be very good at analysing spreadsheets. Most spreadsheets add up better and faster than most managers. Although the numbers may be correct, the thinking often is not. Dealing with spreadsheets is about good thinking, not good maths.

Many spreadsheets are constructed backwards from the bottom right-hand corner; that is where the desired outcome usually sits. If the spreadsheet is meant to deliver a 15% margin, or a

£10 million profit, then the result is always going to be 15% or £10 million, plus a little bit to be on the safe side. We use the spreadsheet to change the assumptions until the correct answer is achieved.

Reviewing spreadsheets requires challenging the thinking, not the numbers. There are three questions you should always ask, listed below.

1 The venture capitalist's question

Who is behind this spreadsheet? Trust the spreadsheet as far as you trust the person who is behind it. A B-grade spreadsheet or proposal from an A★ manager who always delivers is worth far more than an A★ spreadsheet from a B-grade manager. If you are the person presenting the spreadsheet, it makes sense to have some A★ managers lined up to support you. Borrow their credibility.

2 The banker's question

These are the classic 'what if' questions where you get to test sensitivities and assumptions in the spreadsheet. Start with the big assumptions: margins, growth, market size, costs, capital required. Do not bother about details such as the cost of the coffee machine (unless your business is selling coffee machines) – they will not make or break the analysis, even if you can prove yourself very clever by showing that such small assumptions are inaccurate.

3 The manager's question

Every manager of a function or a business will know the key ratios and critical numbers for their part of the business. Philip Green, the British retailing billionaire, can look at a rack of clothes and accurately cost and price them at first glance. You will know the critical budget numbers for your business. Check the spreadsheet to see whether the numbers reflect the reality you live with. If the numbers appear to come from a different planet, start asking some probing questions.

None of these questions requires numeracy, they require clear business thinking. Ask the questions well and people may start to think that you are the king or queen of the spreadsheet, even if you hate numbers.

Chapter 40

Act the part

I t is not enough to do the right things, you have to act the part as well. Style counts as well as substance. This may seem unfair, but success is not always fair. In reality, we all judge others not just on what they do but on how they are. We remember good and bad bosses we have worked with as much for how they behaved towards us as for what they achieved.

Leadership is a performance. As one CEO put it: 'I still get angry and frustrated, but over the years I have learned to wear the mask. I let the team see the leader I want them to see. Most of the time I want that to be positive and supportive. If I need to inject some urgency, some tension, I do so deliberately. Don't let emotion get in the way.'

If you are going to act the part, it pays to know what your role requires. Your role splits into two parts: universal requirements of all actors/leaders and specific requirements of the play/firm in which you are acting. The universal requirements of leaders can be thought of as professional guard, the minimum you must deliver at all times as a leader.

> If you are going to act the part, it pays to know what your role requires.

Developing professional guard

Imagine you go to a meeting. You arrive on time. The person you are meeting arrives 15 minutes late and is badly dressed. He puts his feet on the desk and spends most of his time checking and replying to his text messages while you are trying to talk to him. How will you react? The chances are, you would not be wildly impressed. It is possible that there are very good reasons why this person is behaving like that – he may be having an urgent crisis elsewhere and he may be doing you a huge favour by still finding time to see you. But still, you probably would react better to a more professional approach.

> Professional guard is not just about setting standards for yourself, it is about being a role model for others.

Professional guard is not just about setting standards for yourself, it is about being a role model for others. It also makes it easier for others to deal with you – you do not want them distracted by your behaviour or appearance.

When firms start setting out what they want from professional guard, the result is rarely inspiring or helpful. You are likely to be presented with a box-checking exercise which deals with hem lines and ties. Set your own higher standards by following the Golden Rule: treat others as you would be treated. Here are some of the categories for you to think about:

- How do other people around here really annoy me? Do I want to do the same or set a higher standard?
- Who are the people I most respect and why? What can I learn from how they act and do I want to be like that?
- Dress code: how do people two levels above me dress? Do I want to be seen as part of that group or another group? Dress is tribal: it shows where you belong.
- Meetings: what are the rules of conduct – timeliness, contributions, etc.?

- Emails, texts and phone calls: how soon should I reply and how formal or informal should I be? Typos, emoticons?

- Gossip and banter: as with other forms of communication, assume that the person you least want to hear what you say hears it.

Professional guard in action

I was taking the train from London to Newcastle. On a table nearby I heard a team talking about a meeting they were going to. They were pitching some advertising and they knew it was not up to scratch. There had been a crisis with their creative types who had not delivered. They were working out how they could get the client to go along with what they had cobbled together at the last moment.

They did not realise that they were talking about a meeting with one of my colleagues. I duly reached the offices before they did. They then had a mysterious 15-minute delay before their meeting, while I briefed my colleagues on what I had heard. Ninety minutes later, the advertising agency left looking ashen faced: they had just lost their contract.

Sharing confidences in public is not good professional guard.

There are two great errors in dealing with professional guard. The first is to reduce it to a manual and a box-ticking exercise. As a leader, you should hold yourself to much higher standards than the minimum requirements of a manual. The second great error is to accept the culture of people immediately around you. If your colleagues dress poorly or gossip and bad mouth other colleagues, you do not have to follow their example. By setting a higher standard, you can stand out in a positive way. At worst, accepting the cultural norms means you can land up accepting unethical or illegal standards, as we have been finding in the continuing banking scandals around LIBOR fixing, foreign exchange fixing, PPI mis-selling and much more.

Learn your part

Beyond the general rules of professional guard, you have to work out the specific rules of your organisation. As you ascertain these norms, you have to decide how far you want to follow them. If you find you do not like the cultural norms, you may be in the wrong organisation. Even if you are the CEO, you will find it hard to change the culture. When a great leader joins a lousy organisation, it is the reputation of the organisation that remains intact.

> Even if you are the CEO, you will find it hard to change the culture.

Here are some of the norms you may want to think about:

● Risk: should you take risk or minimise risk?

● Adaptability or conformity: follow the process or adapt to conditions?

● Walk or run: is this a high-paced or a more deliberative organisation?

● Action versus analysis: what is the right balance between doing and thinking?

● Big picture or detail: what is the right balance?

● Customer service or profit maximisation: in a crunch, whose interests come first?

The only right answer is what works in your world. In aircraft manufacturing, lives depend on delivering precision perfectly. In teaching, there is never a perfect lesson – with 30 children in the room, you have to learn to adapt fast and think on your feet. You do not have the luxury of time to deliver the perfect plan.

Chapter 41

Be the part

Acting the part is about how you are, at least to the outside world. Being the part is about who you are. The best leaders not only act differently, they think differently. Continuing leadership research is showing that the way the best leaders think is consistent. There is a distinct pattern of success which we can all learn from.

At first this sounds daunting. If we have to change the way we think, that implies we have to change who we are. We may as well train a tiger to be vegetarian: we cannot change who we are. Fortunately, nothing so radical is required. We do not have to change who we are, we simply have to be the best of who we already are.

> We simply have to be the best of who we already are.

The best leaders in business, education, sports, the public and private sectors share the same seven mindsets:

1 Aim for the stars: the power of high expectations.

2 Be brave: accelerate your career.

3 Stay the course, while others fall by the wayside.

4 Stay positive, not hokey.

5 Believe in yourself, or no one else will.

6 Learn and grow.

7 Be ruthless, selectively.

On a good day, we probably can aspire to all of these. The difference is that the best leaders stay like this every day for years and take each mindset to an extreme. We may not go as far as the top leaders, but we can learn from them. Just as we may not become a world-star sportsman or musician, learning the basics can set us apart from our peers. This section shows how you can grow your success mindset.

Aim for the stars: the power of high expectations

No one starts out with low expectations. But over time we slowly compromise – we settle for what we can. This is a recipe for contentment, but not achievement. The best leaders do not compromise on expectations for themselves or their team. They want to stretch themselves and others. They put the words of poet William Blake to the test: 'You never know what is enough unless you know what is more than enough.' Be prepared to take yourself to the limit, because you do not know your limits until you have passed them.

> The best leaders do not compromise on expectations for themselves or their team.

Aim for the stars

He was the CEO of a successful not for profit, but knew he could do far more. He had been working on education in the UK, but decided to address education globally. He saw that most global education initiatives were well meaning but patronising – smart Westerners would go and tell the locals what they should do to their education system. He had a better way: go to places like India and Uganda and tell them that they were doing great things in education. All he would do was find those islands of excellent ideas and excellent people, and create a movement of teacher change makers who could change the whole system.

It was a crazy pipe dream. He had no money, no team, nothing. And to chase his dream he would have to give up his secure job. He started, but after the first year, his major funder made a strategic decision to pull out of funding any projects in India. Yet he followed the IPA agenda – he had a great idea and built a great team around him. With a great idea and a great team, he was able to drive to action and find the money to support the dream, even after his main funder pulled out.

Two years later, he was helping 200,000 teachers in Uttar Pradesh, was running a successful programme across Delhi and was establishing a new programme in Uganda.

What's your dream?

It is often easier to make big ambitions come true than to make small ones come true. If you have a small idea, no one will be interested. The CEO or government ministers do not have time to spend on small ideas, they need big ideas that will make a big difference. With a big idea, you have a chance to make a difference; to get support from the most powerful people; to inspire and motivate your team.

Be bold: dare to dream.

Be brave: accelerate your career

We all have dreams, and they die as the dawn rises. There is always a voice in our head telling us not to take risk, to avoid embarrassment or failure. It is a persuasive voice, which conjures up countless demons. Because of that our dreams remain as dreams, not reality.

The challenge is to tame the voices of caution that whisper in your ear. You cannot ignore these voices – even the most self-confident leaders have their moments of doubt. You have to deal with them. Here is how:

● **Focus on the prize**. See your future perfect: this is the Idea part of the IPA agenda. It is the dream you want to chase. If the prize is big enough, it is worth taking some risk to gain the prize.

- **Take small steps.** This can be as simple as taking advice, finding some supporters and working up the idea. You do not need to risk everything at once. This is the 'P' part of the IPA agenda: build a team of people who support you and will help you refine your 'I', your idea.

- **Imagine the worst.** Then work out how to deal with it. If you risk looking like a fool, that is not the worst thing that has happened to anyone. If you risk your job, could you find another? Confront your demons, don't hide from them.

Move to action, the 'A' part of the IPA agenda. Find some early wins, build momentum, build confidence. The adage that the first step is the hardest rings true. But once you create a bandwagon, it will start to live a life of its own. Then be bold: be ready to scale fast. Follow the motto 'Think big, start small, scale fast.' Don't bail out too soon, don't settle for a modest win. If you have a future perfect, keep driving to that.

If you are brave you will accelerate your career – you will succeed fast or fail fast. But as we shall see, the best leaders are often in denial about failure. They see temporary setbacks from which they learn and grow stronger. In other words, they have deep reservoirs of resilience to draw on.

Stay the course, while others fall by the wayside

The difference between failure and success is often no more than persistence. James Dyson famously worked through more than 5,000 prototypes before he perfected his bag-less vacuum cleaner. Churchill had to endure his wilderness years between the two world wars when he was seen as little more than a maverick. Abraham Lincoln had two business failures, eight election losses and one nervous breakdown before he became President of the United States.

Telling someone to be more resilient does not help them. Here is how you can stay the course longer:

● **Focus on your future perfect**. Keep your final success in mind and keep driving to it. Stay true to your purpose and your mission.

● **Build your network of support**. It is hard to succeed alone. Find people you can trust, who can make things happen and who can give you advice, comfort and support when you need it. The adage that a problem shared is a problem halved rings true.

● **Enjoy what you do**. Any great endeavour takes great effort. We can all work hard for a while, but you cannot sustain the required level of effort year after year unless you enjoy what you do. Getting to the top of sports, music or business takes endless effort and practice. You only excel at what you enjoy.

● **Focus on the positives**. This is the mantra that coaches repeat whenever their team has suffered a humiliating loss. There is a reason for this. Even in great setbacks, there is much that you can learn. If you learn from each setback, you come out stronger. To paraphrase Nietzsche: 'That which does not kill you makes you stronger' … provided you learn and grow from the experience.

● **Face the brutal facts**. Don't hope that problems will vanish, deal with them. Unrealistic optimism quickly leads to despair. The more you face up to problems, the more experience you gain and the better you will become at dealing with them.

● **Take control**. Crises separate leaders and laggards. Occasionally, the outlook will be bleak. It is easy to feel overwhelmed and give up. But even in the bleakest times, there is normally something you can do. Even if you can do only one thing, do it. If all you can do is make a phone call, then make that call. By moving to action, you create opportunities and hope. You can keep going while others give up.

You will always have good reasons for giving up: work/life balance, finding yourself on the wrong end of corporate politics, bad luck and major setbacks. Everyone endures these challenges. The difference comes in how we choose to deal with each challenge. If you choose to drop your vision of your future perfect, make sure you have some alternative vision you want to chase. It could be as simple as raising a family. Whatever it is, make sure it is something you really want to do.

Stay positive, not hokey

Let's make this simple: do you want to work with or for someone who is always complaining, negative and miserable? Or would you prefer to work with someone who is optimistic, positive and energetic?

Being positive is much more than remembering to say 'Have a nice day' to people. Telling people to be positive is as helpful as telling them to be happy. You can fake being happy or positive by following the corporate script, but that is different from being happy or positive in yourself. Yet being positive is important. The academic evidence shows that people who are positive live longer and better than those who are not.

Live longer, live better

The landmark study involved nuns, who are very useful for such studies. They share the same diet and same routines, so most of the variables are accounted for. On entry to one nunnery, each nun was asked to record why they wanted to become a nun. Some duly wrote that they felt the call of duty and wanted to serve God. We can call this group the 'duty' nuns. The other group expressed their delight and excitement at having the chance to join the nunnery. We will call this group the 'fun' nuns.

Roll forwards 60 years or so and the researchers found that at age 85, 90% of the fun nuns were still going strong, while only 34% of the duty nuns were still alive and doing their duty. On average, the fun nuns lived 9.4 years longer than the duty nuns.

We all see the difference between positive and negative people quickly. Typical symptoms include those outlined in the table.

Positive people	Negative people
Focus on opportunities	Focus on problems
Embrace change	Cling to the past
Support colleagues	Complain about colleagues
Drive to action	Hide in analysis
Take responsibility	Spread the blame
Have high energy	Are passive, have low energy
Are enthusiastic	Are cynical

On good days, we can all be positive. Bad days are the true test of a leader. Simply telling someone to be positive does not help. But knowing that you have a choice about how you behave and how you are seen does help. Keep the table of positive and negative people in mind next time you have a bad day, then choose how you want to be.

Sustaining a positive outlook year after year is harder. As a leader, we are more likely to attract followers and

> Bad days are the true test of a leader.

supporters if we are positive, not negative. I was brought up to believe that either it was raining or if it was not raining, then it must be about to rain. So I have had to learn optimism and learn to be positive. It is a never-ending journey of discovery. Here are some of the ways you can discover the sunshine in your life:

- **Count your blessings.** Try this exercise. Count all the bad things that happened to you today – traffic snarl-ups, irritating emails and annoying news items. It is a quick way to feel bad. Now do the opposite. Find the first good thing to happen in the day – waking up in a warm bed surrounded by all the conveniences of modern life which are beyond the dreams of our recent ancestors is not a bad way to start. From health and dental care, to cars, computers, television and more, we are a very lucky generation.

- **Confront your negative thoughts**. As a simple exercise, wear an elastic band on your wrist. Every time you have a negative thought, lift the band and let it snap back onto your wrist. Use the little shock to challenge your negative thought and find an alternative way of looking at things. You will soon have a sore wrist and a new, more positive way of looking at your world. You will find that most negative thoughts are not necessary. Often the best challenge to a negative thought is to ask, 'So what do I want to do about it?' Either you drive to action, which is positive, or there is nothing you can do about it, in which case there is not much point in worrying about it.

- **Choose your feelings**. If you have had a bad day and someone comes along and is unpleasant, you have every right to feel angry and upset. But there is no law that says you must feel angry and upset, that is your choice. Every time you feel angry, use the elastic band trick again to challenge your emotion. When you realise you can choose how you feel, it is rare to want to feel bad.

- **Focus on the future**. Dwelling on the past is dangerous. Either we look back to a mythical golden past which was better than today, or we look back at all the disappointments and setbacks. Either way does not help us. If we look to the future and then take small steps towards creating it, we give ourselves and our teams hope, purpose and direction.

Believe in yourself, or no one else will

You can delegate most things, but some things you cannot delegate. If you are not enthusiastic and energetic, do not expect anyone else to be enthusiastic and energetic for you. If you do not believe in yourself, no one else will believe in you either. Self-belief matters because it defines what you can and cannot do.

If you believe you can or cannot do something, you are probably right. If you believe you can do it, you will rise to the challenge. If you believe you cannot do it, you will find that is a self-fulfilling prophecy. This matters.

> ## If you do not believe in yourself, no one else will believe in you either.

Talent or self-belief?

We set up a charity to develop great head teachers for schools in challenging areas. About half of our intake was male, half was female. After four years we found that nearly all of our participants who had found headships were male. This was a surprise, because we knew from our internal evaluation data that there was little or no difference in performance and capability between the sexes.

At first, we put this down to the usual suspects: unwitting sexism, lack of good role models and the challenges of child care which still fall mainly to the mother. But we also interviewed as many people as possible who were involved in the process to find out whether anything else might be going on.

We found that the men applied for headships when they (and we) thought they were perhaps only 50% ready. They were confident that they would learn on the job and that they could blag their way past a school selection panel. The women wanted to be nearer 100% ready to take on such huge responsibility. But the truth is that no one is ever 100% ready for the step up to the top post, it is always a shock.

We then found that if men were rejected, they blamed the myopia and folly of the selection board. They were still confident that they would succeed, and would apply for more posts. Typically, the women reflected more deeply on rejection – they assumed that the selection board had made a rational decision and that they lacked some key skills or

▶

experience. They stopped applying for posts until they had remediated their perceived weaknesses.

The imbalance has now been addressed and the female heads are at least as successful as the male heads. The talent difference does not exist, but self-belief will accelerate your career.

Here are some dos and don'ts for building your self-confidence:

- **Focus on your ability to learn, not to do**. If you wait until you have all the skills to take on a new role, you can expect a very long wait. If a new role offers you the chance to grow and to learn skills which you want, then go for it.

- **Build on your strengths**. No leader gets ticks in all the boxes. Everyone has weaknesses and that is why leadership is a team effort. Focus on what you are good at and build a team around you to do the rest.

- **Learn to turn setbacks to your advantage**. The more you take risks, the better you become at judging them and at dealing with the risks that don't work out. For instance, if you ask for a promotion or pay rise you may get it, which is a win. If you are refused the promotion or pay rise, at least you can then set up a discussion about 'What do I need to do to get the pay rise or promotion that I deserve?' Either way, you win. If you don't ask, you are relying on the goodwill of your bosses for your future.

- **Don't look for praise**. The quick way to gain praise is to focus only on what you are already good at. This lets you excel in your comfort zone, but it means you will take less risk and you will learn and grow less.

- **Don't worry about your peers**. Everyone likes to project a positive self-image. From the outside, your peers may look successful and talented. It is easy to feel daunted and inferior as a result. The reality is that everyone struggles with ups and downs, has failures and successes. Define yourself on your own terms, not in relation to others.

● **Don't take criticism emotionally**. Criticism feels like rejection and it is always a shock. The natural reaction is unhelpful: defensive and emotional. Instead, seek understanding. Why have they made the criticism? Even if the criticism is unfair, there will be a reason why you have exposed yourself to that threat. Then focus the discussion on what you can do differently and better – look forwards, not back. No one is perfect, ever, so criticism is your chance to learn, adjust and grow stronger.

Learn and grow

We saw in the introduction to this book that the rules of survival and success change dramatically at each level of an organisation. When you start out, you have to prove yourself by doing things yourself. On becoming a manager, your world should have changed. Instead of making things happen yourself, you had to make things happen through other people. That is a completely different skill set. And as you become a more senior leader, the stakes rise. Leaders have to take people where they would not have got by themselves – they have to make a real difference, not just administer a legacy that they inherit.

The quick route to obscurity is to stick to your comfort zone. If you have a specialist skill, you can have a fine career by being excellent in that skill, but you will not be a leader. Even with a specialist skill, the chances are you still have to learn and adapt. Today's skills are unlikely to be tomorrow's, even if they have not been replaced by technology or offshored to

> The quick route to obscurity is to stick to your comfort zone.

a cheaper part of the world. Average job tenure in the OECD is ten years – you will change employer several times over a 40-year career and your new employer wants current skills, not old ones.

If you want to lead, you have to keep on learning, growing and adapting. That means we have to escape our prison of success. Don't get caught in your comfort zone. Learning means taking risks.

Who's the idiot?

We went skiing and were complete novices. The instructor told us to 'bend ze knees' and we did, as we cautiously tried the simplest ski turns. There was one idiot who fancied himself. He wanted to learn the fancy turns. The instructor tried to help him, but it was a farce. The idiot kept on falling over every time he tried. At least his antics kept us amused.

Slowly but surely, we began to master the basic turns and ventured out onto the blue (easy) runs. We felt pretty pleased with ourselves. Meanwhile, the idiot was nowhere to be seen. Then, at the end of the week, we were going down an easy run when we spotted the idiot. He was hurtling down a black (difficult) run at speed and in full control, using the fancy turns he had so painfully learned. He had risked failure and mockery, we had not. He had learned, we had not. We chose not to think about who the idiots really were.

Over the long term, learning and growth are about taking risks, stretching yourself and exploring new opportunities. But you can also learn and grow in your daily practice by constantly reviewing key events in the day. Use every difficult conversation, meeting, important call or presentation to learn and grow by asking yourself two simple questions: WWW and EBI.

- **What went well?** This is important in both success and setbacks. When we succeed we assume that is the natural order of events. It is not. Catch yourself doing things well and understand why it went well, then you can do more of it and success becomes less random. Even in setbacks, there will have been some things you did well. Learn from them before you beat yourself up too much on what you did wrong.

- **Even Better If.** The evil twin of WWW is What Went Wrong: that is the starting gun for the blame game from which nothing is learned. EBI is an easy way of teasing out what you can do differently and better next time.

Using EBI and WWW is unlikely to produce eureka moments. But it will yield a constant stream of small improvements, which add up to a transformation over time. Think of it as kaizen for professionals.

You can do EBI and WWW at any time – sitting in your car, walking between meetings, whenever you have a quiet moment. If you want to help your team raise their game, it is a positive and action-focused way of debriefing with your team after any key event.

Be ruthless, selectively

There is a dark side to leadership. Leadership is not about being nice to people all the time or trying to win a popularity contest. There are times you have to be ruthless. All the leaders I interview hate being called ruthless, but they are. Even the leader who fired a colleague she had known for 25 years (the two of them had even gone on family holidays together) denied she was ruthless. She saw herself as simply doing what was required for the mission.

Weak leaders compromise. They will settle for the 'B' team. They will accept all the reasons why something cannot be done. When you accept excuses, you accept failure. Strong leaders do not compromise on the mission, and that means they are ready to make difficult and unpopular decisions. Respect, not popularity, is the currency of leadership.

> When you accept excuses, you accept failure.

There are two areas where you have to be unreasonable:

- Setting goals and budgets, and sticking to them.
- Building the 'A' team.

Setting goals and budgets, and sticking to them

If leadership is about taking people where they would not have got by themselves, then it follows that you have to stretch and push your team. You will not settle for the easy target and the easy life. When things get tough, do not revise the goal downwards – work out what more you need to do to achieve the goal. Although you may be unreasonable about the goal, you have to be flexible and supportive about how the team reaches the goal.

Building the 'A' team

The instinct of most leaders is to work with the team they have, support them and help them achieve their goals. This is the right instinct. But you must also be ready to move people out. Normally, this happens for one of four reasons:

1 **Skills and role mismatch**: a new mission or a restructuring simply makes some positions redundant.

2 **Lack of trust**: teamwork depends on trust, and if trust breaks down, one side has to go. The team member goes because leaders rarely fire themselves.

3 **Wrong values**: the wrong values can be like a cancer to the morale and performance of the team. Cut out the cancer before it spreads.

4 **Mediocrity**: few people are outright incompetent. Everyone has the occasional disaster, which is not an excuse to fire them. Much more common is the low achiever who has survived in post because no one wants to make the difficult decision. If you can afford to carry such people, you may also duck the decision. But if your mission is important and stretching, your team will not thank you for having to carry deadweight with them.

Beyond reason

Philip II ran a tin-pot state on the very edge of Greek civilisation, Macedonia. In an attempt to look civilised he hired the rock star philosopher of the day, Aristotle, to tutor his son and heir. Philip II got assassinated and his son, Alexander, took over at the age of 20.

Alexander had ideas above his station. He did not want to prove he was civilised. He wanted to conquer the entire civilised world. Any reasonable person would have told him that was not possible. Thirteen years later, he had achieved the impossible, reached Afghanistan and founded twenty cities that bore his name.

Today we remember Alexander the Great, not his obscure cousin Alexander the Reasonable. The world is not changed by reasonable people.

Some people are naturally ruthless and unreasonable. They are often the psychopaths who will do what it takes to succeed: trampling over the lives and careers of colleagues; leaving morality and ethics to people they regard as wimps. They are not great role models, except for wannabe dictators. That is why you need to be ruthless and unreasonable selectively, not all the time: pick your battles well.

Being ruthless does not mean you have to be unpleasant. What you do may be ruthless, but the way you do it should respect your team. Nevertheless, being ruthless and unreasonable does not come naturally to most of us. It comes over time – we learn that compromise means missing targets, letting down our team and ourselves. It is not worth it. Ultimately, leaders

> What you do may be ruthless, but the way you do it should respect your team.

learn their hard edge from having an important, worthwhile and stretching goal to chase. Such goals rarely permit compromise; you have to do the tough stuff. If you want to achieve something worthwhile, you have to find your hard edge.

Unreasonable leadership in action

1 **Be unreasonable**

Set stretching goals. Force business not as usual. Take people beyond their comfort zone so that they can grow and develop. Focus on impact.

2 **Be flexible about the means**

Do not micro manage professionals. Believe in your team. Let them come up with a better approach than the one you first thought of. If they want help and guidance, let them ask for it and then provide it.

3 **Build the 'A' team**

Do not settle for second best – look beyond skills to find people with the right values and commitment.

4 **Empower and support your team**

Set up your team for success – give them the right budget; give them air cover from politics, interference and administrative grief; ask them what they need and make sure they get it. Pre-empt any excuses.

5 **Be specific and detailed about your expectations**

Be precise about your goals. Specify in detail what good looks like, be clear on timings and milestones. Avoid any vagueness or ambiguity, and check your team understands your expectations. No surprises.

6 **Manage By Walking Away (MBWA)**

Do not solve all their problems for them. Help them learn to step up to each challenge by coaching them, not instructing them.

7 **Monitor appropriately**

Trust your team and they will respond. Do not over-monitor. Review progress early on so that you can take corrective action in time and coach as needed. Break large tasks into bite-sized chunks, which can be achieved, monitored and delivered.

8 **Accept no excuses**

When you accept excuses, you accept failure. But be generous in your praise and do not hog the limelight. Give recognition. Motivate your team.

9   **Deal with setbacks promptly**

Setbacks are an excuse to work better and more creatively, not for delay or scaling back ambitions. Create an open culture where setbacks are recognised early, and you learn from them and drive to action fast. Avoid the blame game.

10   **Drive to action**

Avoid analysis paralysis. Be clear about what happens next and do it now.

Conclusion: the leadership journey

The message of this book is simple: anyone can learn to lead, and to lead better. You do not have to wait until you are given a big promotion to start leading. You can, and should, start leading whatever your position is today. Leadership is not about your title, it is about what you do.

> Leadership is not about your title, it is about what you do.

There is no great mystery about what the best leaders do. Ultimately, they all have the same agenda: the IPA agenda of Idea, People, Action. If you have a good idea about how you want to build a future perfect firm or unit, you have made a good start. A good idea gives you an agenda, which starts to give you control over your destiny, rather than being shaped by external forces. Then surround yourself with a great team and help them turn the idea into action.

The leadership agenda is simple to state, but hard to practise. No one has all the skills to make it happen, and many of the best leaders have very obvious weaknesses. This should be reassuring to you. No leader gets ticks in all the boxes. You do not need to become the perfect leader to succeed, because the perfect leader does not exist. Instead, build on your strengths and be the best of who you are. Leaders come in many styles and flavours – develop the style that works for you and then put the IPA leadership agenda to work.

Instead of seeking perfection as a leader, seek improvement. The best leaders are always learning and growing. You have to do this because what is expected of you changes at each level of the organisation and you will always face new challenges. This means leadership is a journey of discovery, not a destination. Treat it that way: take each new challenge as an opportunity to learn, to grow and to shine.

> Take each new challenge as an opportunity to learn, to grow and to shine.

By having the courage to lead, you will be leading life in Technicolor and with the record button on. That is a good way to live. Your highs and lows will be memorable and you will grow stronger from them.

Let yourself enjoy your leadership journey. You only excel at what you enjoy; only when you enjoy what you do can you sustain the effort required to succeed over many months and years. Your journey to leadership will be unique to you. Whatever your journey is, enjoy it.

Index